G 95

D1207213

# Sports Illustrated
# CANOEING

# THE SPORTS ILLUSTRATED LIBRARY

BOOKS ON TEAM SPORTS

| | | |
|---|---|---|
| Baseball | Football: Defense | Ice Hockey |
| *Basketball | Football: Offense | Pitching |
| Curling: Techniques | Football: Quarterback | Soccer |
| and Strategy | | Volleyball |

BOOKS ON INDIVIDUAL SPORTS

| | | |
|---|---|---|
| Badminton | *Running for Women | *Women's Gymnastics |
| *Basketball | Skiing | I: The Floor Exercise |
| *Bowling | Squash | Event |
| Fly Fishing | Table Tennis | *Women's Gymnastics |
| *Golf | *Tennis | II: The Vaulting, |
| Handball | Track: Running | Balance Beam and |
| Horseback Riding | Events | Uneven Parallel Bars |
| Judo | Track: Field Events | Events |
| *Racquetball | Wrestling | |

BOOKS ON WATER SPORTS

| | |
|---|---|
| *Canoeing | Skin Diving and Snorkeling |
| Powerboating | Small Boat Sailing |
| *Scuba Diving | Swimming and Diving |

SPECIAL BOOKS

| | |
|---|---|
| *Backpacking | Safe Driving |
| Dog Training | Training with Weights |

*Expanded Format

# Sports Illustrated
# CANOEING

BY DAVE HARRISON

Photographs by Dave Harrison and Tom Ettinger

**HARPER & ROW, PUBLISHERS, New York**
Cambridge, Hagerstown, Philadelphia, San Francisco,
London, Mexico City, São Paulo, Sydney 1817

Picture Credits

Dave Harrison: pages 10, 12, 14, 15, 16, 19, 21, 43, 44, 48, 50 (bottom), 56, 57, 60, 61, 68, 76, 88, 91, 105 (bottom), 106, 109 (bottom), 111, 115, 117, 120, 122, 125, 128, 133, 136, 138, 140, 154, 155, 159, 161, 164, 169, 171, 174, 178, 180, 182, 185, 189

The Mariners Museum, Newport News, VA: page 18, top

The Public Archives of Canada: page 18, bottom

All other photographs by Tom Ettinger

Diagrams and illustrations by H. Russell Suiter

The map on page 141 was drawn by Stephen Gussman and appears in *New England White Water Guide* by Ray Gabler, copyright © 1975 by Ray Gabler.

*Designer: C. Linda Dingler*

Library of Congress Cataloging in Publication Data

Harrison, Dave.
  Sports illustrated canoeing.

  1. Canoes and canoeing.   I. Sports illustrated
(Time, inc.)   II. Title.
GV783.H38   1981      797.1′22      80–8687
ISBN 0-06-014853-5             AACR2
ISBN 0-06-090874-2 (PBK.)

    83 84 85 10 9 8 7 6 5 4 3

# Contents

# Acknowledgments

This is a book about canoes and canoeing, the product of my lifelong love affair with a craft that is a genuine North American invention. Kayaks, rafts, dories, and rowing boats can duplicate some of the functions of the canoe, but none possesses the canoe's versatility. In form, only the kayak could be considered a sibling.

Sharing my love of canoes and canoeing is my wife, Judy, who patiently assisted in researching and organizing the material for this book. To Lee and Judy Moyers, proprietors of Pacific Water Sports in Seattle, who provided both expert advice and equipment, and to Ulrich and Nono, and to Steve, paddlers extraordinaire, we extend our thanks for their support.

# Introduction

## From the Arboretum to the Arctic

I have the good fortune to live in Seattle, a city perhaps more abundantly blessed than most with both natural and manmade refuges for recreation. From the windows of my commuter bus, during four or five months of the year, I can see couples paddling among the serpentine channels of the University of Washington Arboretum. Several channels extend under the freeway, whose columnar supports create a surrealistic slalom course. Not far away, in fact, suspended between two diverging branches of the freeway, is a complete set of actual slalom gates, a practice course for canoers and kayakers from the university.

Beyond the protected channels of the arboretum and the security of its concrete wilderness lies a lake, where, thanks to farsighted city planners, forty-foot powerboats, sailboats large and small, wind surfers, hydroplanes, and canoes coexist on pleasant, unpolluted waters. Into this larger world venture forth those canoers who have advanced beyond the hesitant strokes of the more timid paddlers in the arboretum. They catch my eye. Surely, the same confidence and curiosity that lures them onto the broad expanses of the lake is a giant step toward further exploration by canoe. While greater mastery and broader horizons are

11

Urban settings can provide a variety of canoeing adventures.

More remote environments will lure the experienced canoeist.

worthy goals in any sport, there is equal value in the pleasures and relaxation enjoyed by those who go no farther than the lily pads marking the outer boundaries of the arboretum.

Perhaps the canoe's greatest virtue is that it makes larger a world which in most other ways is becoming ever smaller. Inquisitive canoers can spend an entire afternoon of exploration and discovery in the arboretum, which my rush-hour bus races past in a few moments. A continent away, in New Jersey, the most densely populated state in the nation, one can canoe for hours in the relative solitude of the Great Swamp or the Pine Barrens. I once spent seven hours there, winding my way down one of the piney rivers with a family group and seeing only one other person—a kayaker. Well, that's not quite true. One mile from our destination we passed under a wooden footbridge and were greeted from overhead by some walkers, who asked where the river went. "To the ocean" was our simple reply.

All rivers share this common destiny. And both the river bound for the Arctic Ocean after a trip of a thousand miles and the one that meanders toward the Atlantic through the pine barrens in the shadow of metropolis are suitable for enjoyment and exploration. Adventure is where you find it, and only time and appetite should limit the extent of one's journeys. I am as fascinated by the bird- and wildlife inhabiting a suburban slough as by the lush, dripping canopy of an Olympic Peninsula rain-forest river, or the foaming cataracts of a remote and seldom-traveled wild river in northern Canada.

Urban adventures are possible as well. In the United States, as in Europe, canals and waterways still exist whose commercial use is long since over but whose populated banks tell you a hundred stories. City parks, arboretums, or lakes surrounded by houses and condominiums also invite exploration. There is something appealing about canoeing that usually brings forth a friendly response from those into whose territory you might stray.

There are no age barriers in canoeing. Young and old alike can share its many pleasures.

Canoeing can be an end in itself: a Sunday paddle, a picnic, two hours' escape. Or it may be strictly for exercise. It is a more serious activity for canoers who graduate to the world of white water, pitting themselves each weekend against precipitous rivers, or for those who thrive on competition and enter the varied events of competitive canoeing—marathons, wild water, slaloms, or even poling. For many, the ultimate is the canoe trip or expedition, conjuring up nostalgic visions of Indians and early explorers.

Canoeing is both an activity in itself and a means to the enjoyment of other pursuits. Because it glides unobtrusively into places accessible in few other ways, the canoe is often the vehicle of choice for photographers, fishermen, artists, geologists, birdwatchers, historians, and prospectors. The canoe becomes your magic carpet to remote nooks and crannies, as you will find yourself becoming photographer, fisherman, geologist, ornithologist, and historian as well.

The chapters that follow will introduce you to the canoe, and the skills it requires, before going on to explore some of the possibilities and frontiers of canoeing, so that you may follow your own vision of the sport, whether your destination be the arboretum or the arctic.

Birdwatching and wildlife sighting may be your reason for canoeing, but for the young people above the canoe is the perfect craft for fishing.

# 1

# A Boat for Every Occasion

Like the wheel, the canoe of the Algonquin Indian has been improved only slightly by technology, and those improvements have been in the materials used rather than in hull forms or principles. No other craft, except possibly the Eskimo kayak, combines so well the elements of speed, maneuverability, lightness, and load-carrying capacity. The dugouts of the Kootenay Indians were magnificent boats that made the best use of available materials, the huge trees in the forests of the Pacific Northwest, but they lacked the flexibility of design to become all-purpose craft. The flat-bottomed pirogue of the Louisiana bayous looks like a poor man's canoe, but simplicity of construction from available materials to serve fishermen on still waters justifies its existence.

## Early North American Watercraft

The predecessor of the modern canoe could only have been invented in the northern forests, where the gums, natural sinews, and, critically, the canoe birch stood ready to provide the materials for a boat that could be built on the spot without a single nail. It is remarkable that ribs steamed to shape along a keelson, set in a form of wooden

17

Wood and canvas, the canoer's equivalent of Chippendale.

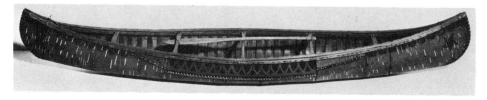

Malecite canoe.

stakes, planked longitudinally, and covered with birch bark could so effectively merge attributes of hull speed, strength, weight, and displacement in a design that would survive through the centuries.

In the eighteenth and nineteenth centuries, the canoe achieved its penultimate form in the Montreal and North canoes, which bore the loads of explorers and voyagers who, in their pursuit of the fur trade and other commerce, drew the map of Canada and found their way to the Pacific and Arctic oceans. The mighty Montreal canoes, 35 to 40 feet in length, carried a crew of fourteen and were capable of holding loads of almost three tons. These *canots de maîtres* were used on larger bodies of water, such as the Great Lakes and the St. Lawrence River. At Grand Portage on the western shore of Lake Superior their cargo of supplies bound for the interior posts was exchanged for furs brought in smaller North canoes by brigades from the interior of Canada.

*Canot de maître,* or Montreal canoe, shooting the rapids.

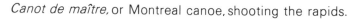

Despite their size, the formidable loads, and the rugged routes they traveled, these workhorses of the fur trade were fragile craft, held together by threads of watape, especially the root of the red spruce. The bark covering was made watertight through gumming with pine pitch, a repair that had to be undertaken frequently, en route. The journals of early fur traders such as Peter Pond, David Thompson, and Alexander Mackenzie make constant reference to this discouraging interruption. Mackenzie, in his successful westward journey to the Pacific Ocean, was forced to abandon his torn and waterlogged canoes at the Fraser River in British Columbia and finish the journey overland.

## The Modern Canoe

About one hundred years ago, the direct descendant of the Indian birchbark canoe and forerunner of the modern lightweight canoe was crafted in Canton, New York, by J. Henry Rushton, whose classic Nessmuk model was 10½ feet long and 27 inches wide and weighed only 18½ pounds. This cedar boat was of lapstrake construction, the planking individually planed and butted to be completely watertight. In his later canoes, Rushton incorporated some economical design features, which others had begun to develop by stretching a canvas covering over a hull of wooden ribs and planking. The watertight integrity of the newer craft was the result of technology rather than the painstaking craftsmanship required in the all-wood canoe.

The traditional wood and canvas canoe is the product of painstaking hand labor.

In 1902 the Old Town Canoe Company was incorporated, and to this day their wood and canvas canoes (more recently, the canvas has been replaced by fiberglass) set a high standard of workmanship. Ironically, this construction, which superseded the prohibitively expensive all-cedar construction of the early Rushtons, seemed for a time to be itself threatened, not through any deficiencies of performance or change in hull design but by economics. Old Town's fine wood canoes are a product of highly skilled hand labor and can take eight weeks or more to complete. Fortunately for the traditionalist, these beautiful canoes have enjoyed a renaissance in recent years despite their ever-increasing price.

## CANOE DESIGNS

Before worrying about materials, let's look at today's hull shapes and purposes. Start with the logical assumption that a wide, flat-bottomed canoe, with the width carried well into the ends, will be slow but initially stable, while a long needle-nosed hull with a deep, narrow cross section (deep V'd) is going to be fast, hard to turn, and unstable (at least in the hands of an inexperienced paddler).

### Stability and Maneuverability

The question of design becomes more complicated when you discover that this flat-bottomed canoe, while stable in quiet waters, may become quite unstable in heavy seas or white water. It may also be a revelation to learn that a longer greater-volume boat will handle more easily than a shorter small-capacity boat. A 15-foot canoe is *not* easier to handle than a 17-foot canoe. Once you put two people and 150 pounds of gear into the smaller canoe, the increased load causes it to sink farther into the water. Now you have to move the canoe against a greater volume of water, producing the same kind of friction that slows the forward momentum of a wide, flat-bottomed canoe.

### Length

Most recreational canoes for two paddlers will be 15 to 18 feet in length. This is true whether they are used for canoe tripping, white water, or pleasure cruising. Solo paddlers may prefer the low end of this range, but most are just as happy in a 16½- or 18-foot boat. In fact, there are few applications for which a 17-foot canoe is not suitable. Therefore, add or subtract 6 to 18 inches, depending on the uses and loads to which the boat will be subjected. Canoes in excess of 18 feet are often the choice of expeditioners to provide comfortable load-carrying capacity. Whether loaded or not, there are other factors to be considered by the performance minded. Other things being equal, a long canoe will be faster than a short canoe because canoes are governed by the physics of *displacement* hulls. That means that speed will equal 1.55 times the square root of the waterline length. Thus the maximum or potential speed (displacement speed) of an 18½-foot canoe is 6.7 miles per hour; a 15-footer, 6.0 miles per hour.

## Keel vs. Keel Line

A boat with a high rocker bottom—one with a pronounced curve from end to end, like a chair rocker—will turn quickly, whereas a long straight keel line—whether the boat has an actual keel or not (and increasingly they do not)—is designed for speed rather than maneuverability. Keel "line" describes the rocker or presence or absence of a V, and it is these design characteristics that affect a canoe's quick-turning and tracking properties (the canoe's tendency to glide in a straight line). A keel may provide some degree of protection, or be a part of a canoe's structural integrity, but in the absence of other hull characteristics, its contribution to tracking capability is slight. And in white water or fast-moving rivers a keel is a downright liability.

This high rocker boat is designed for fast turning.

Canoe hulls (from left to right, aluminum, ABS, fiberglass, and wood) reflect a variety of requirements as well as the design limitations of the material.

Only the aluminum canoe (rear) has a keel. Of these recreational canoes, the extended keel line of the fiberglass (second from foreground) suggests a faster hull.

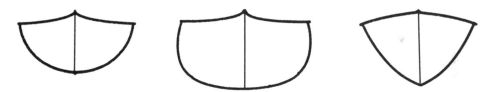

Round, flat, and "V"-bottomed hulls.

The endless ingenuity of designers and manufacturers in blending different cross sections, bow curvatures, and keel lines has created a variety of hulls for every conceivable use or combination of uses. The pictures provide only a sampling. Simply combining two or three elements fails to tell the whole story, since factors such as length, width at the gunwale (the upper edge of the canoe's side), width at the four-inch waterline (an arbitrary point of measurement to determine tumblehome—described below), depth, and, more importantly, how far into the bow and stern certain of these elements are carried, must also be considered. As an extreme example, a deep-V hull (normally associated with fast boats) used with a snub-nosed bow and stern would be about as fast as a hollow log.

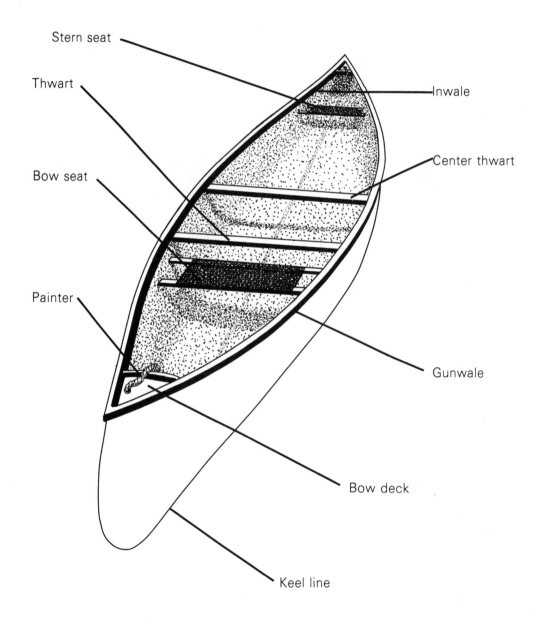

## Capacity

How much a boat holds obviously depends on length, but depth at center, width, and fullness at the waterline (sometimes referred to as "tumblehome") also affect capacity. Since a common standard is lacking, you should consult your dealer for capacities of specific boats. A well-designed recreational canoe suitable for a wide range of cruising, canoe tripping, or white water should hold between 650 and 1,000 pounds of paddlers and baggage. There should be at least 6 inches of the canoe's side showing between the level of the water and the upper edge of the boat when it is fully loaded. This is known as the freeboard. Less than 6 inches of freeboard is unsafe.

## What to Avoid

Perhaps the best way to learn about design is to discuss the features you *don't* need until you reach a point, or use, where a certain design element will make an important difference in your canoe's performance (such as for heavy white water, slalom or flat-water racing, or solo paddling).

First, avoid the extremes, whether they are flat-bottomed, round or deep V'd, or highly rockered. A long keel line combined with a V hull is OK for cruising, but avoid it if you plan to paddle in winding rivers or even moderate rapids.

Generally speaking, avoid canoes of less than 16 feet in length or greater than 18½ feet; canoes with less than 35 inches or more than 37 inches of width at the gunwale line amidships; or less than 13 inches in depth. These all suggest an extreme design, or purpose, that is inappropriate for most recreational canoers.

Avoid canoes that weigh too much—over 80 pounds. (There has never been a canoe that weighed too little!) And, finally, don't go for the lowest-priced canoe. With its versatility and long life, an $800 canoe is a bargain when compared to most other watercraft—or, in fact, to most recreational equipment.

## CANOE MATERIALS

As the number of canoers grows each year, so does the impetus to develop advanced designs and new materials to meet their increasingly sophisticated requirements. Currently there are half a dozen different materials used for canoe hulls: wood, aluminum, fiberglass, Kevlar 49, and various other plastics.

## Wood

The case for wood canoes can be made on entirely aesthetic grounds, for they are objects of beauty and warmth. Sufficient hull designs exist in wood to meet all but the most specialized uses, and the modern wood canoe's durability has been enhanced by combining it with other materials, including fiberglass, resin oil, and improved canvas fillers, so that a well-constructed wood canoe has strength-to-weight characteristics that compare very favorably to some of the newer materials.

Because of the lead used in canvas fillers (and no satisfactory substitute has yet been developed), some manufacturers, because of health regulations, are substituting fiberglass for canvas. Unfortunately, this results in a canoe that has the hard "feel" of fiberglass at the expense of the creaking, soft "feel" of the wood and canvas which many of us had come to love. That softness also meant the ability to absorb sharp blows, to which the old canoes were surprisingly resistant.

If you should have a chance to lay your hands on an old-style wood and canvas canoe, it will, if properly cared for, last a lifetime. The wood canoe does not stand up to mishandling and reckless technique, and of course it requires more maintenance than the newer models. Nevertheless, having paid a premium for the canoer's equivalent of the Chippendale, the owner of a wood canoe should find its maintenance a labor of love.

Aesthetics alone could make the premium-priced wood-strip canoe your choice.

# Aluminum

Until recently, aluminum canoes outsold all others by a margin of three to one in the United States. At the same time, wood canoes were the largest sellers in Canada. Today, approximately 60 percent of the canoes in the United States are aluminum (though there has been a steady decline in their percentage of new sales). They are durable, lightweight, and inexpensive, and their standard designs provide for a wide range of recreational uses. Produced in volume with a limited number of hull shapes, aluminum canoes were created for mass-market use and have been for many years the staple of outfitters and canoe liveries. Aluminum is definitely a material that merits the canoe buyer's serious consideration.

All aluminum canoes are not created equal, and construction methods, quality of temper, thickness of the aluminum skin, and hull shapes differ from manufacturer to manufacturer. Price—you tend to get what you pay for—and manufacturer's reputation are probably your most reliable guides.

No canoe is indestructible, but the best aluminum canoes come close. Without question, they are the most carefree. Because of the hull-forming and riveting processes in aluminum canoe manufacture, there are definite limitations in design. But the most popular 17- and 18-footers represent only a modest performance compromise, when the factors of durability, utility, weight, and price are considered.

Some people complain that the aluminum canoe is too cold or too hot, and too noisy, and that it sticks to rocks. To others, aluminum is just plain unappealing. However, if utility and longevity are more important to you than appearance and feel, go for aluminum.

# Fiberglass

A good fiberglass canoe will compete favorably in price with other synthetics and with wood, and, depending on the design and manufacturing method, provide very satisfactory weight-to-strength characteristics.

A "good" fiberglass canoe, however, is dependent on many factors, the most important being the quality and method of "lay-up." This refers to the number of layers of fiberglass cloth used in its construction. In general, more layers are better. There are as many varieties of lay-ups, resins, and molding and curing techniques as there are manufacturers, including the innovative craftsman who turns out a canoe a week in his garage. A good fiberglass canoe is not a mass-produced item but represents many hours of hand labor. The mold can embody the most exacting refinements of the canoe builder's art to achieve the optimum performance for that canoe's intended use.

Unfortunately, there are also a number of pirates—those who have knocked off someone else's hull design by making a mold from an existing canoe —and there are all too many ways to cut corners in materials and construction. I would recommend that prospective buyers avoid the more cheaply produced sprayed or "chopper gun" canoe in favor of the hand-laid-up fiberglass boat.

The buyer of a fiberglass canoe must exercise much greater care and put a good deal more faith in the dealer or manufacturer than when buying a canoe of any other material. Since the subject of fiberglass construction is reasonably complicated, you would be well advised to shop for a fiberglass boat—in fact, any canoe—at stores specializing in canoes, as opposed to sporting goods stores carrying everything from fishing tackle to bowling balls. You should also ask experienced canoeing friends or folks in your local kayak and canoe club for guidance. If you do not go for a major brand name, these people are likely to have strong opinions about some of the smaller producers who may be turning out boats for your local or regional market.

## Kevlar 49

This is the name of a Du Pont aramid fiber (originally developed for tires) now being woven into cloth. Although similar to fiberglass cloth, Kevlar has a greater tensile strength and is more resistant to tearing and abrasion. Like fiberglass, and sometimes in combination with it, Kevlar is laid up in a mold, impregnated with resin, and usually finished off with a smooth outer layer called the gel coat. You may pay 30 to 40 percent more for a Kevlar boat; however, I have seen them in action—and in very rough going—and I am a believer. To many, the price is justified by incredible strength-to-weight proper-ties. Indeed, one exemplary Kevlar canoe, although only 16½ feet in length, 35 inches wide, and 15 inches deep, is capable of carrying almost half a ton of people and gear. It weighs just 60 pounds and can withstand the severest punishment to which a canoe might conceivably be subjected. There are some newer canoes designed for expedition paddling that weigh as little as 40 pounds.

From the manufacturer's point of view, Kevlar is a difficult material to work with, and that, along with its premium price, has restricted the number of companies offering such a craft. Kevlar is no guarantee of a quality product, but a builder using it is likely to be in the forefront of canoe technology.

## ABS Royalex

Royalex is Uniroyal's name for a multilaminated sandwich of vinyl and ABS
—acrylonite-butadiene-styrene—with a closed-cell foam core. Old Town calls
it Oltonar. Other canoe manufacturers use either the Royalex name or their
own; while the hull-forming process may be proprietary to a particular manufacturer, they use basically the same material.

What's unique about ABS Royalex? The molecularly cross-linked vinyl
provides a durable surface, the ABS offers penetration resistance, and the foam
gives backbone (plus flotation) to an otherwise sloppy laminate. These features
produce considerably more durability than fiberglass, while not being as expensive as Kevlar. In addition, the foam core in the laminate gives the material its
own flotation—as opposed to aluminum or fiberglass, where flotation must be
built in or provided. (Wood, of course, also provides its own natural flotation.)

Those are the good qualities of ABS Royalex, but for the purist the
thickness of the laminate means a weight penalty and limitations on the sharpness of line. You just cannot get the same fine, cut-through-the-water bow in
ABS Royalex that you can in fiberglass or Kevlar. Nevertheless, it appears to
be the material most directly competitive to aluminum in providing good
all-round recreational hulls that are virtually indestructible and reasonably
priced.

## Polyethylene

One manufacturer, under the brand name Ram-X, has come up with a thermo-
formed, high-density polyethylene craft that tests the limits of indestructibility.
It is also the best-selling canoe in the United States at this writing. At present,
however, the material requires some sort of superstructure to give the hull
rigidity. This means a weight penalty and a certain awkwardness. Yet, like
aluminum, there is a cost advantage, and no doubt there will be polyethylene
boats in the future which overcome present design deficiencies.

## THE RIGHT BOAT

Earlier in the chapter we talked about what to avoid in selecting a canoe. Now
it is time to inject *you* into the equation. Consider that every material or design
represents some kind of compromise or trade-off. However, where you live, how
you vacation, how often you expect to canoe, and the type of available water

inevitably will point toward the most suitable craft for you. A family canoe is going to be a different boat from the one with which you expect to do some serious racing, and yet there are a number of designs that are just as appropriate for canoe tripping with the kids as for use in white water.

The canoe design and material that meets your highest and most likely use is the right choice. For people living in Illinois, it would make little sense to purchase a boat with a high rocker and white-water capabilities if they are only planning to use their canoe locally, just as it would be a waste of money to buy a Wonacott, cedar-strip canoe, or Jensen racer to keep tied to your dock on Half-Acre Pond.

## Suitability Table

There is no canoe built that cannot be put to some use for which it was not designed, and fortunately there is enough overlap in design and materials capability to enable one canoe to meet a number of requirements. The table opposite takes a stab at correlating materials, designs, and use; however, it is one man's perception, and there will be exceptions in every case. Aluminum-canoe enthusiasts may insist, for example, that there are special races *just* for aluminum canoes and argue that they are the only white-water boat; so be it.

The absence of a check mark in some cases does not indicate unsuitability, only that I would have other preferences.

## Shop for Value

One more thought on price and its corollaries: Unless your canoe is destined for only the most occasional use, buy the best canoe you can afford. Yet be conscious of design and canoer acceptance. There is always room for individuality, but owning a canoe with an oddball shape or tacky workmanship will detract from your full enjoyment of this sport.

If you try to buy a good used canoe, you will discover that they hardly exist. By the same measure, your well-chosen canoe of good manufacture should never depreciate in value if reasonably maintained.

## CARING FOR THE CANOE

Fortunately, most canoes require little or no care, the exception being the wood canoe, which you buy with the thought that you will revel in its care and

The absence of a check mark in some cases does not indicate unsuitability, only that I would have other preferences.

| | Pleasure | Family | Canoe Tripping | White Water | Flat-water Racing | White-water Racing | Utility (camp or group use) |
|---|---|---|---|---|---|---|---|
| Aluminum | x | x | x | | | | x |
| Wood | x | x | x | | x | | |
| Fiberglass | x | x | x | | x | | |
| Kevlar | | x | x | x | x | x | |
| ABS or Poly | x | x | x | x | | x | x |
| Flat bottom | x | x | x | | | | x |
| Round bottom | | | | x | | x | |
| Deep V | | | | | x | | |
| Shallow V | x | x | x | x | x | | |
| Straight keel | x | x | x | x | x | | x |
| Moderate rocker | | x | x | x | | x | x |
| High rocker | | | | x | | x | |
| Under 75 pounds* | x | x | x | x | x | x | x |
| Over 75 pounds | x | | | x | | | x |

*There was never a canoe that was too light, but you may not wish to pay the premium for a lightweight boat if your intended use is occasional or utilitarian.

maintenance. I can think of no piece of recreational equipment that is so forgiving of neglect and whose performance is so unaffected. (Imagine, if you will, the ten-speed bicycle whose derailleur or chain goes uncleaned or unoiled for two years.) This is not an invitation to sloppiness. A sense of tidiness and pride of ownership will usually motivate canoers to clean the sand and grit from inside their boats, massage the abrasions on their fiberglass boats with acetone, or wax the hulls of their aluminum canoes. But unless a boat must be kept to some performance standard for racing, or unless forward motion, comfort, or portaging weight are affected, maintenance is more a matter of choice than necessity.

Canoes, regardless of material, tend to sustain more injuries on dry land or within three feet of shore than in all the white water in the Americas, usually as a result of being dropped, dragged, rammed, or tramped in while sitting on land. My canoe trips have taken me and my boats into some of the ruggedest canoeing environments on earth, but disabling accidents have been few and far between, and most of the injuries sustained have required no more than a piece of duct tape to repair. Remember that the first canoes were constructed in the forest. Seats, thwarts, gunwales, and decks can all be fashioned out of local materials, if need be.

Duct tape makes a good temporary patch. Just be sure the hull surface is dry before applying.

# Wood

Wood and wood-canvas canoes obviously require a good deal more attention than other boats, but they are a lot more resilient than most people realize. The former Chestnut Canoe Company in Canada told of a canoe owned by a Mr. Kennedy, the first member of Parliament from the Yukon Territory, who in 1963 contacted the Chestnut factory to ask if they would canvas and refurbish his 16-foot Prospector—used on the Yukon during the Klondike Gold Rush of 1898 and in steady use ever since.

If you are going to own a wood canoe, your loving care for it will be directly proportional to the premium you paid and your recognition that this object of beauty requires more than a kick in the ribs from time to time. Fortunately, many of the newer wood canoes have been treated or fiberglassed to be more resistant to moisture, puncture, and cracking than the earlier wood and wood-canvas models. To the extent that wood is exposed, because of age or injury, its principal enemies are sand and grit and moisture. The first two act as abrasives and will add weight by working their way into the cracks and the wood grain itself. Moisture also adds weight and, over time, may lead to rot.

At a minimum, wood canoes should be hosed out periodically, or swamped in lake or river to flush out the sand and grit. A sponge can finish off the job and get out the excess moisture. During the off season, a light sanding followed by a coat of marine varnish will prolong the life of the wood surfaces. If you sand the old coat carefully, you will minimize additions to the boat's weight. Less frequently, canvas will have to be sanded down and a new coat of paint applied, preferably sprayed on. Torn canvas is easily repaired, using a fiberglass patch. I have effected semi-permanent patches, under way, by cutting a patch out of a bandanna, slipping it in between the canvas and the wood planking, and filling in the torn area with airplane cement. Later, a couple of licks of paint on top made the patch almost unnoticeable.

# Other Repairs and Maintenance

The most vulnerable areas of a canoe tend to be in its underbelly, just ahead of the stern and just behind the bow. On rocks and under heavy use, even the toughest materials begin to wear thin here. Aluminum is probably the least affected. As ABS Royalex has gradually made inroads with the livery and outfitting people, they have found it necessary to epoxy Kevlar "bang plates"

Resin, catalyst, fiberglass cloth, and a cheap paint brush are all you need to make a permanent repair to a fiberglass canoe. All are available in hardware and automotive stores.

to the vulnerable bow and stern areas in order to extend their canoes' life. You can do the same. Or, if you are not a stickler for looks, applying multiple layers of duct tape to these areas will help.

Having patched your canoe's injuries with duct tape while on the river, you will eventually tire of looking at them and decide to put on a more permanent patch. Most hardware, automotive, or marine stores carry fiberglass cloth and cans of resin (with their companion catalyst) and, except for the mind-warping smell, it is an easy matter to follow the directions on the can and make a permanent patch. You will need a piece of cloth, a coffee can in which to mix resin and catalyst, a cheap paintbrush (it will have to be thrown away after one use), and sandpaper to clean and roughen the area to be patched. A temperature in the seventies and good ventilation are important. Kevlar canoes can be patched with fiberglass, or you can obtain special patching materials from your dealer.

Putting a hole in an aluminum or ABS canoe is a feat in itself, and duct tape will suffice for temporary repairs on these as well. Permanent repairs require more specialized attention than can be covered here. That's the time to call the dealer.

If your aluminum canoe sustains a major or minor dent, a good semblance of the original shape can be recouped with a well-placed kick to the damaged area, or, if more precision is called for, a few adroitly placed strokes with a rubber mallet or a sock filled with sand. The same is true of ABS Royalex, which also responds well if warmed. In fact, ABS has some "memory," and a major dimple received on the river in the morning may well pop out after your canoe sits tied on top of your car in the sun for fifteen minutes.

Many paddlers like the feel of a wood paddle.
The bent shaft on the left is preferred by racers.

# 2

## Paddles, PFDs, and Appurtenances

Having chosen your canoe, you have made your toughest decision and perhaps a compromise, as well. Choosing paddles is much easier and there is plenty of room for experimentation. Other accessories for the canoer involve minimal cost or are easily improvised.

## PADDLES

A paddle is a simple device. Those used by the Indians in their dugouts and canoes were nothing more than wooden poles with one end hewn to some semblance of flatness. Up to a few years ago, most paddles for recreational purposes were made of ash, spruce, or maple, and, except for regional eccentricities of blade shape, they were only a modest improvement over the native originals. If you can still find one of these in a good straight-grained wood, they make fine all-purpose paddles, but avoid the "popsicle sticks" sold in sporting goods and boat stores—usually stacked in a barrel and meant to be emergency tools for motorboaters.

The paddle does represent an extension, in every sense of the word, of you, the paddler. Let

37

your paddle selection be an ego trip, if you will, but remember this: Any paddle of good quality will do the job.

## Wood Paddles

Today, synthetics have largely replaced the one-piece ash or spruce paddle, but you can satisfy your aesthetic cravings with one of the handsome laminated wooden paddles on the market. A good laminated paddle is lightweight, strong, and warm and has a spring—or flex—that many paddlers find pleasing, especially over long distances. Costing $20 to $75, and laminated from selected woods, they can weigh as little as 1 or 2 pounds. To compensate for a thin profile or the use of lighter, softer wood, more laminations or a single layer of clear fiberglassing and a metal or fiberglass tip are added for reinforcement. The grips are of two types, the pear and the T. The former is generally used for cruising and the latter for racing and white water.

## Synthetics

As you might suspect, the durability and variety of the synthetics makes them increasingly popular. Unfortunately, some are popular because of low price and are even cruder implements than the Indian originals. One should be prepared to pay $25 or more for a good synthetic paddle. It will have a blade of epoxy,

White-water paddlers prefer a T grip, but for most paddling, the shape of the grip makes little difference.

Synthetic paddles come in a variety of shapes and materials. Durability might be the reason for choosing one.

fiberglass, or Kevlar, with a tempered, round, or oval aluminum shaft, covered with plastic to minimize the conductivity of heat and cold. My own preference is for a polyester or fiberglass shaft (hollow, like a fishing rod) that has some flex—that is, the feel of wood—and with a blade that is durable and yet as thin as possible. There are some epoxy blades that will withstand the roughest white water or canoe-tripping treatment without a tip protector; other blade materials need this protection. For most synthetics, T grips seem to be the overwhelming favorite, but now the variations on the T are so numerous that only your hand will be able to make the decision. For 90 percent of paddling, however, the shape of the grip is of little consequence.

## Other Designs and Materials

More exotic designs are available to the specialized user or the equipment freak; the bent-shaft paddles originally designed for marathon and flat-water racing are one such example. Usually made of fine laminated woods, and very expensive, they are promoted by some ethusiasts as being easier to use, providing a greater forward reach and a smoother, faster stroke while reducing the porpoising (bobbing) tendency of a canoe under a full head of steam.

Still newer paddles, using Kevlar 49, epoxy blades, and fiberglass shafts, finely tapered, have attempted to test the limits of weight reduction, weighing in at under a pound. The theory is that over long distances, in which a day's canoeing might involve no less than ten thousand strokes, you will need less cumulative energy or muscle power to propel the canoe. It makes sense, but the trade-off, of course, is that such a hummingbird wing cannot be used to pole your canoe upriver or away from the beach, kill rattlesnakes, or double as a filleting board.

## Paddle Length

What about paddle length? One outdoor writer has quipped that, just as Abe Lincoln suggested a man's legs needed to be long enough to reach the ground, so a canoe paddle should be long enough to reach the water. The canoe tripper who will be taking long leisurely strokes, standing up in the canoe to survey the rapids and using the paddle as a pole from time to time, should choose a paddle which, when stood alongside on the floor, reaches to eye level or higher. The white-water and slalom enthusiast, on the other hand, will favor a paddle that is almost a foot shorter than chin-high. Until experience or a specialized requirement dictates otherwise, a stern paddle of chin height and a bow paddle six inches shorter will be comfortable for cruising of all sorts. For white water, you may wish to take a couple of inches off that.

## LIFE PRESERVERS (PFDs)

Since 1971, the wearing of a Coast Guard–approved Personal Flotation Device (PFD) has been a matter of law, and with more and more people taking to the water, it's a good one. Brightly colored for good visibility, the PFD should be thought of as an article of clothing, like a ski parka or tennis shorts. In hot weather it can be worn with a bathing suit; in the cold, it acts like a down vest under a windbreaker or rain parka. And although its integrity as a life preserver may suffer ultimately, it makes a great cushion for sitting or even lying down at the lunch stop.

Look for a United States Coast Guard–approved Type III life jacket of either tube or panel construction. Avoid the "horse collars," which tend to chafe the neck and lack, in the case of cheap, non-USCG-approved models, sufficient flotation or adequate protection against rocks. The panel-type life jackets, usually filled with PVC foam (Ensolite), are somewhat more comforta-

Canoers should don life preservers (PFDs) as a matter of habit.

ble, but a number of models have a tendency to ride up in the water, in some cases dangerously so.

My own preference is for the tube type, filled with blocks of polyethylene foam and with a tie around the waist.

Getting the right size is important. Not only do you need sufficient flotation for your weight—and this should be indicated on the label—you should try the vest on for overall comfort.

Type III PFDs are a compromise between comfort and safety, since most will not keep an unconscious person fully face up in the water. The Coast Guard apparently reasoned that, in order to encourage canoers to use them, they would permit designs that would be worn cheerfully and comfortably. Your PFD should keep you in a semi-vertical position in the water, provide protection from the rocks, and not be a hindrance when swimming.

I have paddled a few miles in my life without a life jacket, and undoubtedly so will you. The Coast Guard can hardly be lurking behind every bush along every waterway, nor does every situation demand a PFD. Good judgment will suggest, however, that younger children, white-water boaters, and nonswimmers should always be protected. Keep in mind that a PFD can compensate only for your lack of buoyancy—not for your lack of common sense.

## APPURTENANCES

With canoe, paddles, and life preservers you're ready to go—that's the beauty of canoeing.

A few other items are useful but not obligatory; as always, utility should be your primary consideration.

### Lines

Whether tying up to a dock or a tree for a picnic or hauling the canoe up a riverbank, some good sturdy line is a necessity. Bow and stern lines are called painters. A few yards are probably adequate for most short jaunts; a canoe tripper might be wise to carry up to fifty feet.

### Sponge and Bailer

A sponge is a good companion, even for paddling on a millpond when the sun is shining and your boat is completely leak-proof. Somehow, a little water

An old bleach bottle makes a great bailer. Note extra flotation for white-water paddling in this canoe.

always manages to collect in the bottom of your boat, whether off the paddle tip or brought in when you launch, and having a sponge quickly takes care of this annoyance. If you are going to be out in the elements, and certainly if there are going to be some rapids, both a sponge and a bailer are in order, conveniently tied to a thwart. Any large household sponge will do, although I have seen specially designed foam sponges, covered with terry cloth and with a small loop sewn on one corner so that it can be tied to a small line—a nifty idea. An old bleach bottle cut to form a scoop can bail a couple of inches of water out of a boat in no time, is practically weightless, and costs nothing.

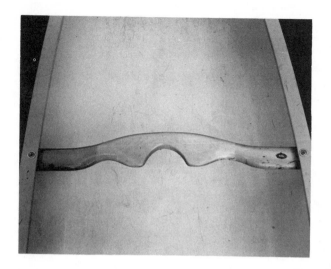

Carrying yokes can either be the commercial variety (above), permanently fitted midships in your canoe, or makeshift (right), using paddles tied in place. Life preservers or other padding can be used for carrying comfort.

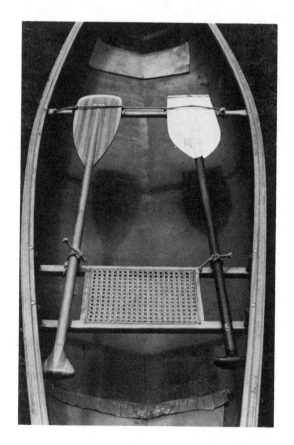

## Carrying Yoke

For carrying the canoe alone you will want a carrying yoke. You may either install a commercial variety or improvise with some nylon or cotton sash cord, using your canoe paddles and stuffing life preserver, sweater, or poncho between the cord and paddle blades to cushion the shoulders. For twenty years my canoes have had their little cords in place. This system has the added dividend of getting the paddles to wherever you are going without having to carry them separately.

## Knee Pads

If you are going to be doing any white-water or extended canoeing, permanent or semi-permanent knee pads should be installed. Any closed-cell foam or neoprene can be used, cut into 10-inch squares and cemented into position with epoxy or contact cement. Temporary pads can be merely taped in place with duct tape. Paddlers of aluminum canoes, where adhesion is a problem, often wear painter's knee pads, which can be bought in any hardware store. For fussier folks, there are commercially available knee pads, or you may wish to carve form-fitting cups out of ethafoam blocks and cement them into your canoe.

## Duct Tape

Canoers and white-water boaters, in particular, have come to depend on duct tape to such an extent that it is, as often as not, referred to as "boat tape." Since the tape has many other uses besides patching or protecting, it is probably all you'll need for most excursions, although my own kit also contains wire and a few nuts and bolts. In addition to patching small and large cracks, duct tape can be used to protect a paddle shaft from constant abrasion with the gunwale —and applied to the gunwale as well. It will patch a torn rain suit, broken-down tennis shoe, or broken beer cooler. I once saw two halves of a broken kayak rejoined on the river, and the boat finished the trip!

## Waterproof Packs

Since you are going to be around water, and since you are likely to be carrying something with you, even if it is only your lunch, sooner or later you will need a waterproof bag or pack. The ultimate in canoe design may be reached, but

Waterproof packs come in all shapes and sizes. The bag below features a system of Velcro closures.

the search for perfection in watertight containers is never ending. Clear vinyl envelopes with Velcro enclosures, metal ammunition carriers, war-surplus hard rubber and canvas containers, double air-chambered transparent camera bags, rigid high-impact polystyrene boxes, four-peck rubberized white-water duffel bags, molded fiberglass gunwale-width boxes that take up a quarter of the canoe —these are just a few of the possibilities. After twenty years, I have at least one of each.

For carrying sensitive gear such as cameras, you will want either a rigid or hard pack or box, or one that inflates, so as to be able to withstand impact. The perfect combination of accessibility, durability, and absolute watertight integrity is yet to be discovered, but it's fun to watch the inventor's ingenuity at work. For the time being, I have found the hard fiberglass box, measuring about 18 by 12 by 8 inches deep, with a smaller gasket-lined snap-down lid, to be the most useful camera case for canoeing. I have lined it with foam and, like a jigsaw puzzle, fitted my camera, three lenses, a few boxes of film, and some minor doodads into it.

Fragile items or not, the important considerations will be size or capacity, weight, durability, and reliability and ease of closure. Closures involving plastic sliders or roll-down-and-snap devices seem to seal more effectively than the pleats and tie or zipper arrangements. For the hard packs that use a rubber gasket, check the gasket periodically, since rubber will harden and crack in time.

At any rate, you should have fun seeking your "perfect" waterproof bag. You will no doubt be as successful as the skier who searches for "fog free" goggles.

The two-person carry—on the shoulders.

# 3

# Getting Started

There are a few things you need to know even before you get your boat wet. Unless a canoe is kept tied up at a dock you are going to have to transport it to and from the water. We'll look at some boat-moving options and then learn some basic techniques.

## TRANSPORTING THE CANOE

The canoe is nothing if not portable. Atop a sedan or station wagon, even a foam pad or an old blanket can serve as your "rack" for short distances; just make sure that your padding is under any part of the gunwales that might come in contact with the car.

To tie the canoe in place, use two lines over the top and far enough apart to distribute the tie-down pressure, yet not so far toward bow and stern as to lose their grip. Unless you use a rack, you will have to take the lines completely through the door or window openings.

A rope pulled straight down from both bow and stern to the bumper is OK if the canoe is firmly secured across the hull and if its lateral movement has been restricted. Better yet, form

Even smaller cars can easily accommodate a full-sized canoe. A line
from bow to bumper will be next.

A sturdy rack and taut lines make this
rig possible.

equilateral triangles with a line drawn through the canoe bow to either end of the bumper and the same arrangement at the stern.

A good set of racks is your best bet. It is important to anchor them securely to the car. I speak from experience, having watched two of my prized wood and canvas canoes fly off the top of our car in a vicious side wind. The canoes were properly secured to the racks, but the racks weren't tied fast to the car. Everything flew off the rooftop, teaching me a hard lesson.

The best racks clamp positively and securely to the rain gutters, supporting two- to four-inch-wide crosspieces, with blocks or some other device to prevent lateral movement of the canoe. While I prefer wood crosspieces, some tubular racks incorporate sliding clamps that screw down on the gunwales.

For tying down, use a good sturdy rope—not clothesline—of tightly woven cotton, hemp, or nylon, which permits you to get a good grip and which will hold a knot. Loose lines tend to get looser; there is no substitute for lines as taut and secure as you can make them. Make sure you periodically check these ropes for wear and either replace them or move the knots and friction points from time to time. Perhaps your bow and stern painters can double as tiedowns.

Two, three, or more canoes can be piled atop a car, but with each additional boat you add geometrically to the forces of wind, friction, weight, torque, and vibration brought to bear on your ropes and racks. No matter how many canoes you plan to carry, your objective should always be the same: to minimize slack and movement, be it the rack in relation to the car or the movement of the boats forward, sideways, and up and down.

## The Shuttle

Unless you put into a lake, or a river with negligible current and paddle in a circle back to your point of departure, you are going to need a shuttle, a means of transportation waiting at the end, at your takeout point. For a downriver run or canoe trip of several days, arranging the shuttle may be as challenging as the trip itself. Obviously, you will need either one or more extra cars or a nonpaddling driver.

Because of shuttling, the self-propelled sport of canoeing all too often requires more than its share of gasoline. I have also tried motorbikes, ten-speed bicycles, shank's mare, and my thumb. For long trips, we have hired shuttle drivers to move our cars to a takeout distant from our launch point. More ambitious trips have required trains and float planes. These are all good reasons for joining a canoe club, where you are likely to find people going where you want to go or willing to follow you. Most clubs publish a trip schedule, detailing

For short distances, the two-person carry is fine. For a very short distance, such as dock to water, the carry opposite, using the knees, is OK.

dates, trips, leaders, and degree of difficulty. Through the leader, car pools can be coordinated and shuttle arrangements made.

## CARRYING THE CANOE

For a short distance, it is an easy matter for two people to pick up a 70-pound canoe from each end and move it between car and water or even around a short portage such as at a dam. Use the bow and stern decks as handles or put the end of the boat into the crook of an arm or on the shoulder. The canoe can also be carried for short distances with one person on each side, as long as each person is the same distance from opposing ends of the canoe. (If your partner grabs the canoe by a thwart positioned four feet behind the bow, you will have to grab the gunwale or thwart on your side that is four feet ahead of the stern.)

One person can move a canoe a very short distance by using the knees as both lever and incline. This is especially appropriate for moving a canoe from land, or dock, to water. It is also the first and last positions in the one-person overhead carry.

## One-Person Overhead Carry

The one-man portage is as much a part of canoe tripping as poling is to skiing. So it pays to figure it out and master it, even if your only canoe trips are to a neighborhood pond.

To get the canoe up on your shoulders, start by standing directly behind the midpoint of the canoe, its bottom resting on your knees. Next, put your left hand on the gunwale near you, just ahead of the center thwart, while reaching well down the center thwart with your right hand. Go slowly into a sitting position, knees well bent and your upper body counterbalancing the weight of the canoe, as you pry the canoe bottom up with your knees. At the same time, you will be pushing down on the gunwale with your left hand and pulling the thwart with your right, as you rotate the canoe on your thighs until its open hull is almost facing you and you are able to reach up and grab the opposite gunwale with your left hand. At this point you are holding the upper gunwale with your left hand about six inches ahead of the center thwart. Your right hand moves down to grip the thwart next to the lower gunwale.

Now comes the moment of truth, the clean and jerk. You will sink and recoil upward, pushing up your right hand (the lower gunwale), at the same time pulling down and steadying with your left hand on the left gunwale, and duck your head under that center thwart so it all comes to rest on the back of

A                               B                               C

*One-Person Lift*

Stand at the middle thwart and roll the canoe bottom up to rest against your thighs (A). Reach down and grab the thwart (B) and then roll the canoe around on your thighs (C). With the canoe facing you (D), and the canoe balanced on

your neck. If you are going to carry the canoe more than a short distance, it makes sense to have a carrying yoke, either the commercially carved style or the paddles and padding mentioned earlier.

## Two-Person Overhead Carry

Some canoes have no center thwart—for reasons which elude me—in which case you will either have to install one or resort to a two-person carry. The two-person overhead carry is identical in execution to the one-person carry just described, with the participants at either end of the canoe, but this is one instance where theory and practice collide. While two would seem better than one, by virtue of sharing the weight and eliminating the balancing act, the fact is that for any distance beyond a few yards, one person can comfortably carry a canoe a lot farther than two. More importantly, you won't be making a lifelong enemy out of your seemingly misstepping partner, who invariably goes up when you go down, zigs when you zag, or runs out of steam just as you catch your second wind.

The best compromise and most effective utilization of two persons is to have your partner hold up one end of an overturned canoe while you step under the center thwart. Your partner lowers the canoe onto your shoulders, steadies it, and you take off. At the end of the carry the sequence is reversed.

D           E           F

your thighs, reposition your hands, the upper on the gunwale and the lower on the thwart. Push up with your lower hand and pull down with your upper as you spring up from your crouching position and duck under the canoe (E), letting it come down to rest on your shoulders (F).

## GETTING WATERBORNE

If your ideas of getting waterborne are modest ones, and if you are planning to learn canoeing one stroke at a time, read on. However, if you are already thirsting for the whitecaps of Great Bear Lake or the rapids of the Chattooga River, you would be advised to read chapter 8, "Safety and Fitness."

Your partner can hold up one end of the canoe while you get under and he can do the same when you go to put it down.

Paddling a canoe may be the most natural thing in the world, but getting into and out of a canoe seems to separate the initiated from the tyros. If you have a partner, one should hold the canoe for the other, preferably with the canoe fully afloat. While your partner steadies the canoe, you grasp the gunwales on either side and in front of your seat, step into the canoe, and lower yourself into the boat with most of the weight on your arms, not your feet. If circumstances, including the absence of a partner, require that you enter the canoe somewhere in the center, grasp the gunwales and move yourself forward or backward to your seat, advancing your hands along the gunwales as you go.

This does not mean that the canoe is such a precarious craft as to invariably require a precisely executed embarkation. You will often see able canoeists take all but flying leaps to and from their boats, creating hardly a ripple. But a proper technique should be mastered so that in those situations requiring finesse—such as loading on a windward shore as the incoming surf threatens to dash your canoe against the rocks—you will instinctively use the most conservative moves.

It is generally regarded as gauche to get into a canoe while it is on shore, and for some of the daintier models, including wood, this can put a severe crunch in the hull or backbone. Likewise, a canoe should be loaded while it is fully afloat; never load it on land and then drag it over rocks and gravel to the water.

To enter, grab the gunwales and move to your position as your partner steadies the canoe.

# Getting Out of the Canoe

Another popular life-shortener is to run the canoe up on a beach. Adding insult to injury, some bow paddlers will hop out of the canoe and pull canoe, stern paddler, and all well up on shore; upon which the person in the stern must stand up in the teetering boat and move perilously up the canoe's back, suspended between water and shore. It's better to hold the boat, still fully in the water, as your partner disembarks.

Another common cartoon situation is the exit at shore or dockside in which one or both partners stand up in the boat and reach for the shore as they push the canoe out from under themselves. A variation has the paddler standing up and stepping out onto a shore that is suddenly not there, as the force of forward motion sends the canoe scooting away from shore and the unfortunate tyro into the water, two feet from the riverbank. Even for experienced canoers, getting into or out of the canoe is when you run the greatest risk of getting wet. Whatever the circumstance, there is no substitute for a thoughtful partner to hold the boat for both entries and exits.

To exit a canoe correctly, nudge it up to the bank, have your partner get out and steady the craft as you move forward, keeping low and holding on to the gunwales. (Below) How not to get out of a canoe. Note the precarious bridge between water and bank. This exit risks getting you wet and damaging the canoe as well.

If you have no partner, getting out of the boat calls for getting a good hold on the dock or shore and pulling yourself out, or using your paddle as an outrigger or crutch. A paddle laid across the gunwales, with its blade resting on the bank, can be used to support your full weight as you move from canoe to shore.

## Trim

Now that you know how to get in and out of the canoe, let's discuss two other important subjects—trim and the positioning of people and gear to achieve optimum balance.

Trim refers to the position of the boat in relation to the water. A well-trimmed canoe is absolutely level from bow to stern and from gunwale to gunwale. There are circumstances when a *slightly* bow-heavy canoe is desirable, such as in a side wind, but such adjustments can wait until you have a better feel for canoeing. You will tend to have an efficient craft, under most conditions, if bow and stern are level. The most common problem usually involves an

A trim canoe is most efficient (A). Too much weight in the stern (B) may subject the canoe to windvaning.

A

B

unloaded canoe with a robust stern paddler and a petite bow partner. The canoe will pivot precariously on the rear quarter of the canoe bottom, like a kid doing a wheelie with a motocross bike—an attitude which is unstable and awkward and which can make even the attainment of stable forward motion difficult. Should this unmatched pair find themselves in a good breeze, they have a real problem.

If there is gear or duffel to be loaded, the solution to the problem is easy; equilibrium is achieved by adjusting the load toward the bow paddler. Another solution is to move the stern or bow seat forward.

Even the most unpracticed eye is going to recognize an unlevel canoe, and the solutions for attaining trim are usually obvious. What may be less obvious is the *importance* of a level canoe. If one is going to advance beyond pond paddling, it's as important as tight ski bindings or air in your bike tires.

For a single canoer, trim is best achieved by kneeling in front of the center thwart, with the buttocks resting on it. You should be positioned toward the side on which you will be paddling. Obviously, you will not be trim gunwale to gunwale, but that's the way it works. If you are going to sit, get on the bow seat and face the stern of the boat. By the way, if you are soloing in any but the calmest waters, you will have to get your bow down, either by placing a pack well forward or by kneeling in a position that accomplishes the same objective. It is even tougher for a single paddler to tame a "windvaning" canoe (so-called for the tendency of the canoe, like a wind vane, to pivot on its axis and point directly away from the wind). I've seen novice canoers go in one frustrating circle after another, for just a modest breeze can catch a bow and in a twinkling turn the whole boat away from the wind.

## Center of Gravity

I defy you to tip a canoe over while lying in its bottom. This tells you all you need to know about the importance of a low center of gravity. Not surprisingly, a canoe with duffel on the floor is more stable than an empty canoe. Likewise, kneeling is a more secure position than sitting, and seats that are suspended three inches below the inwales (inside the gunwales) are going to give more stability than ones bolted just below the inwales. A long sleek racing boat tends to have its seats positioned lower, and one designed for tripping will tend to have them higher. The trip boat is likely to have gear as ballast, and its occupants are likely to put a premium on comfort if they will be sitting in a canoe for six hours; hence the higher seats.

The approach, then, is to load people and gear in such a manner as to achieve a trim canoe, with the weight concentrated as low as possible consistent with comfort. If you're going to have passengers, you will want them on the floor, not sitting up on the thwart, but some way should be devised to keep them off the bottom of the canoe. A boat seat or duffel will do the trick. If your passenger is a child, it is imperative to keep his or her behind off the cold bottom of the canoe and out of the inevitable collecting puddle.

Under way, on lake or river, and depending on the inherent stability of the canoe design, I adjust my position to reflect the degree of difficulty of the situation. Most of the time I'm sitting comfortably. But when winds and whitecaps begin to rise, or rapids are approached, my partner and I shift to our knees, buttocks resting against the seat. Not only have we lowered our center of gravity, we have increased our points of contact with the canoe, enabling us to use weight shifts as we both "ride" and control the pitch and direction of the craft.

In very heavy or violent rapids, or should we take in an inordinate amount of water, we will come away from our seats entirely, so that we are kneeling flat on the bottom of the canoe, buttocks on our heels. If you should ship water, particularly in the absence of gear or other ballast, you will find just two inches sloshing from side to side makes a boat intolerably unstable. As uncomfortable as it may be, that's the time to get well down on your knees and get to shore, where you can bail or empty the canoe as soon as possible.

Never stand up in a canoe except when it's necessary and appropriate to

To cope with heavy water, the stern paddler has dropped low on his knees.

Rapids ahead. Standing up in a canoe has its uses.

do so, such as scouting the rapids ahead. Experienced canoers stand up in their canoes all the time, just as bikers ride with their hands off the handlebars, but presumably they have reached the point of proficiency and harmony with their vehicle where virtuosity or the requirements of the situation make it appropriate. Since standing in a canoe violates the low-center-of-gravity principle, you ultimately will have to be the judge as to when such a maneuver is called for. Like every other rule in this book, you should read, follow the instructions, and, when mastery is achieved, make up your own rules. If you accomplish your purpose and do not pitch headlong into the lake, then standing meets the rules of "appropriateness."

It is easier to make a canoe go in a straight line if it is well trimmed and properly loaded. We will cover a multitude of techniques in the next chapters, but you need to know a few other things right now so that you can get the boat on the water. Remember that strokes are presented in sequence. Each level must be mastered before a new technique can be learned.

A                                         B                                      C

## THE POWER STROKE

To get going, you need a straight power stroke. Grasp the top of your canoe paddle palm down, putting your lower hand down the paddle shaft as close to the blade as possible without having your hand in the water. Both bow and stern paddlers should lean forward at the waist and extend their arms. Lead with the lower hand, followed by a forward punch with the upper hand, to put the paddle blade into the water ahead of you on the same side as your lower hand; then pull the boat forward, describing a reasonably straight line with the canoe paddle parallel to the keel line. Bring your upper body back with the paddle blade. If you are in the bow, pull the paddle out as it reaches your hips. In the stern, carry your blade farther back, depending on your need to execute one of the correcting strokes (described later). As the paddle blade comes out of the water, twist the shaft to "feather" the blade (turn the blade surface horizontal to the water to reduce air resistance) for its return and the start of the next stroke.

D

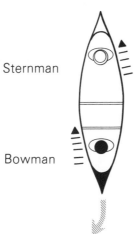

Sternman

Bowman

*The Power Stroke*
This stroke uses both back and arms (A). Paddler punches out with the upper hand (B), pulls the paddle out of the water just past the hips (C), and feathers it (D) for return to the next stroke.

## Which Side?

As with most canoeing maneuvers, going in a straight line is best accomplished by partners who pick a paddling side and stick with it. (In downriver and marathon racing, this is not always so.) Your paddling side is like your throwing arm, but it does not necessarily follow that a right-handed thrower will feel more comfortable paddling on the right. For me, it just happens to be the opposite. Happiness is finding a canoeing partner whose natural side is the opposite of yours. There are plenty of paddlers, however, who have had to become proficient on their other side: usually compliant spouses or intimidated guest paddlers.

Anyway, the rule is to pick a side and stick with it, and the stern paddler should not resort to changing sides in order to make the canoe go straight—or to go in any direction, for that matter. This in spite of the fact that within three strokes your canoe will start veering off to the right if you, in the stern, are paddling on the left, your partner on the right. Why? Because most canoes (unless they are designed to go in a straight line, such as a racing boat) are somewhat directionally unstable, but, more importantly, because your position in the extreme stern of the canoe gives you much greater leverage than the bow

A                                          B

position. Think of the ease with which a tire lug is loosened with a good long-handled tire iron, and you will understand the principle: The paddler in the stern is well out on the end of the lever.

## THE STERN PRY

The easiest and most reliable response to correct and offset this strong tendency of the canoe to veer away from your paddling side is the stern pry, or rudder, also referred to as a pushaway stroke.

At the end of your power stroke, when your lower hand is well behind your seat, put the heel of that hand on the gunwale and turn your upper hand palm outward, in order to pull firmly on the grip of your newly created lever. Your lower hand holds your lever in place on the gunwale, which acts as a fulcrum as you pull the grip toward your chin and "pry" the stern of the boat toward you—thus straightening out the boat.

Only practice and adjustment to your particular boat and bow partner will tell you how often and with what degree of force to apply your lever, but generally you will need to make a compensating stern pry every two to three strokes. Needless to say, a continued or vigorous application of the stern pry will turn your boat sharply toward your paddling side, so that it is more than just a correcting stroke. Some paddlers put the paddle shaft right on the

C

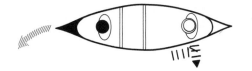

*The Stern Pry*
The stern paddler puts the paddle shaft against the gunwale (A) and (B) pulls the handle toward her, thus prying the stern over (C). The sequence can be repeated or power strokes commenced until a correcting pry is required.

gunwale (rather than using the heel of their hand as a buffer); while this method is a little tough on paddles and gunwales, positive leverage is dramatically increased.

The stern pry is not as classy as the J stroke, which is covered in the next chapter, but the potential force with which it can be applied makes it more dynamic and useful. By adjusting the pitch of the paddle blade—using your upper hand—and varying the vigor of your lever, you can achieve a full range of effects, from a gentle ruddering action to an abrupt directional change and slowing of the boat. Continuing to "push away" with the back of your paddle blade, following a stern pry, will continue to turn your canoe in the direction of your paddling side.

## THE STERN SWEEP

From time to time, because of winds, the current, or your bow paddler's action, you will need to turn your bow more forcefully *away* from your paddling side. This is accomplished by "sweeping" the paddle blade in an arc, slightly fore and well aft of you; your paddle shaft is now extended out over the water, instead of perpendicular to the gunwale, and only a quarter to a half of the blade is in the water. Here again, exerting maximum force near the completion of the arc will sharpen the canoe's response.

A                                                                                          B

## GROUP LESSONS

In recent years clinics for all grades of paddling have sprung up. These are offered by canoe clubs, dealers, community colleges, and outdoor recreation schools patterned after the Outward Bound programs, and while they may range from semi-volunteer operations—such as those offered by local canoe clubs—to slickly promoted productions, they are well worth looking into. Canoeing lends itself to group instruction, and, unlike skiing, no one gets left behind.

While a particular course may emphasize river canoeing, or canoe camping, the good ones will concentrate on teaching judgment in addition to equipment requirements, paddling techniques, and safety practices. The "follow me" or "sink-or-swim" mode of instruction is something to be avoided.

Since the fullest enjoyment of canoeing—as well as the safest—comes from the tandem partnership between family members or friends, learning in a group provides an instant assemblage of like-minded people. Students might range in age from 10 to 60; a good student-teacher ratio is 5 to 1. That means the instructor has one student in his or her boat and must watch only two other boats. A good rule is that no couples, roomies, brothers, sisters, or friends paddle together, and every effort should be made to switch students among

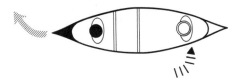

*The Stern Sweep*
The stern sweep starts well out from the boat (A), and gets its maximum power as the blade is pulled toward the stern of the canoe (B).

different boats, different partners, different paddle sides, and each end of the canoe.

The early sessions on pond and pool will emphasize boat control, maneuvering—perhaps even races—among buoys, paddling backward, and paddling sideways. Kneeling at poolside, students may practice sweeps, draws, pries, and, finally, braces. The last are executed in the extreme to see how far they can go before falling in. Tipping over a lot in the canoe is also part of the learning and familiarization process. Dipping the gunwales to see how close they can come to touching the water without actually going over heightens awareness.

Later on the river—if that is the emphasis—an easy but varied stretch will be chosen. Every current, every eddy, every obstacle will be worked and reworked. Perhaps the same one-mile stretch of water will be run several times. Sides, ends, and paddlers will be switched. Getting dumped is part of the drill, and chilly waters make fast learners out of the less gifted. Group dynamics and healthy competition provide additional impetus to the learning process.

For those of us who survived the sink-or-swim school of canoeing, it is gratifying to see these clinics growing in number and popularity. I would strongly recommend aspiring paddlers to seek them out. There is absolutely no substitute for getting wet under controlled and safety-oriented conditions.

# 4

# Skills for Quiet Water

The canoeing strokes I was taught as a kid, and which were depicted in the popular manuals (many of which still survive in print), now appear stilted, a trifle unnatural, and passive. It would have never occurred to me that the paddle could also be used as a powerful lever, as a support for the weight of an entire canoe, or as an outrigger, permitting the negotiating of seas and cascades which in years past would have been avoided by all but the most brash.

Today we think about paddles and strokes in new ways for we know that water can be leaned on, pushed off of, and used to pull a canoe in any direction. Formerly canonized strokes such as the bow rudder and cross-bow rudder will not be found here. Our thesis is that fewer is better and that perfection of the newer strokes and their variations will provide the arsenal necessary for tackling any kind of water.

As you gain proficiency, get out over your paddle; don't be afraid to put your full weight on it. Next, observe the principles of leverage to maximize your control over the boat; apply your paddle-blade power as far from the canoe's pivot point as possible and maximize your grip on the canoe (by kneeling, for example). Use the natural lever

69

Today's strokes are active but natural.

A

B

C

*The J Stroke*

The J stroke starts underwater (A) and both upper and lower wrists are rolled forward (B) so that the power face of the blade "catches" and straightens out the canoe. C and D show blade coming out of the water feathered to return for next stroke. Closeup in E shows wrists rolled forward and power face of paddle pushing away.

of paddle shaft and gunwale. Finally, use your back and upper body, moving your torso forward and backward with your strokes or out over the water for your draws and sweeps.

## Kneeling

While your time on quiet waters will be mostly in a sitting position, you would do well to learn the strokes from a kneeling position. With a lower center of gravity and knee contact with the hull, you are in a better position to make vigorous and positive moves, reaching well out from the canoe on your draws and sweeps without worrying about balance. If you think about paddle strokes as a means of moving the canoe rather than moving water, the leverage advantage resulting from increased contact with the boat becomes apparent. It's the difference between grabbing the jack handle in your fist or using your thumb and index finger. After you've mastered the strokes and absorbed the principles involved, you can get up on the seat and relax.

*Note:* Strokes are described for two canoeing partners, with observations, where appropriate, about solo paddlers in the same situation.

D    E

# THE J STROKE

Up to this point, the bow paddler has been performing a basic forward stroke, oblivious to your struggle, with pries and sweeps, to stay on a straight course. We will commit your partner to this oblivion a bit longer while we push you even farther out into the lake, using a J stroke.

The J stroke is harder to perfect and lacks the power potential of the stern pry, but for quiet paddling and long distances, where a change of pace or a resting stroke is desirable, it is both valuable and pleasing. Unlike the stern pry, which can be executed exclusive of a forward stroke, the paddler sows the seed of the J almost immediately after a forward stroke is under way.

While the stern pry, or pushaway, uses the nonpower face of the paddle blade (that is, the blade facing away from you on your power or straight forward stroke), the J utilizes the power face, which, shortly after you start your forward stroke, is pitched outward through a combination of wrist and paddle actions. Halfway between the start of your stroke and where you reach your hips, roll your lower wrist sharply inward (forward) and drive the paddle deeper into the water as your upper and lower grips coordinate to turn the inside edge of the blade sternward, so that you can pull the power face of the blade up and away from the canoe with your lower arm. The simultaneous

*Stern Sweep and Bow Draw*
The stern sweep as the bow draws will cause this canoe to circle sharply to the left.

downward push and twist of the paddle shaft is the key; you will feel the blade "catch" as it makes its "J." There is a natural transition from the final upward part of the J as the blade is withdrawn from the water, already in a feathered position and poised for the next stroke.

Only with practice and many miles of paddling will this stroke become natural to you, as you unconsciously adjust the motions and the amount of power applied to accomplish a smooth forward thrust.

## STERN SWEEP AND BOW DRAW

It's time to bring the bow into the act. Your most effective stroke is the stern pry; for the bow paddler, it is the draw. The two are antagonistic, as opposed to complementary, so if the bow is to initiate the turn homeward, you can provide a complementary sweep as the bow paddler draws the paddle blade toward the boat, causing the boat to turn *away* from your paddling side.

To execute the draw, the paddler reaches as far out as caution permits, jabbing the paddle blade into the water on the same plane as the keel line and pulling the paddle toward the canoe, making sure to pull it out of the water well before it reaches the canoe. Several jabs and draws by the bow paddler—really, "drawing" the canoe to the paddle—coupled with a stern sweep will pivot the boat smartly. The stern paddler could also substitute a stern draw for the sweep, recognizing that it is the final part of the stern sweep that provides

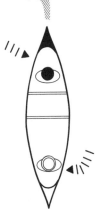

the real turning impetus. The stern draw is the same as the bow draw, but is executed somewhat behind the stern paddler's hips. With experience, you will refine your techniques and develop your own preferences.

The beginner's tendency in the draw is merely to extend the arms and twist the paddle blade, but the grip and orientation of the paddle to your grip need not change. You must turn your whole upper body from the hips and extend both your head and arms out over the water, your eyes on the paddle shaft, to plant the paddle as far out from the boat as possible.

## STERN PRY AND BOW SWEEP

At the stern paddler's whim, or if a turn in the other direction is called for by route or circumstance, the turn may be initiated with the *stern* power stroke —the stern pry. The complementary bow stroke is the bow sweep.

*Stern Pry and Bow Sweep*
The stern pry and the bow sweep causes the canoe to turn sharply to the left. Note bow paddler leaning well forward to get maximum leverage on his sweep.

The bow sweep is much the same stroke as the stern sweep described in chapter 3, but now the bow paddler gains leverage by reaching the paddle tip as far out in front of the boat as possible and "sweeping" the paddle in a broad arc. As with the stern sweep, however, the arc can be shortened so that the principal power is applied as far out on the lever as possible; that is, well in front of the boat.

This stroke—in fact, all the basic strokes—can be used repeatedly to achieve the most punch at the point of maximum leverage in the stroke. Thus the stern may give three or four sharp pries in succession, as the bow paddler jabs the sweep out in front of the canoe, reaching with back and arms to pull the bow around. On the other hand, if your pace is leisurely, you can initiate your turn, and most general-purpose canoe designs, being directionally unstable, will tend to continue it. (A V-hull deep-keeled canoe, however, is going to require a more persistent technique.)

Earlier, we had the stern paddler substitute a draw for a sweep. Likewise, in this complementary pair, the stern may do a reverse sweep as an alternative to the pry. For the reverse sweep the stern paddler uses the nonpower face of the paddle to carve an upside-down arc in the water as the paddle pushes the water away from the stern of the canoe.

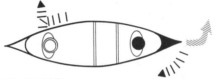

An option: the reverse sweep and bow sweep.

You now have all the strokes you will ever need for quiet waters, and there are legions of canoers who get by on less—such as letting the stern paddler make all the moves! But to advance beyond unruffled waters, you and your partner need to perfect the sweep, the stern pry, and the bow draw and bow sweep, and ideally you will each take the time to learn the other's strokes.

## REVERSE

To this point we have gone only in a forward direction, but your canoe has a "reverse" as well. On quiet water, strokes to reverse direction are seldom needed except for moving away from shore, maneuvering in or out of a tight corner, or docking. Often, "full astern" is accomplished by a good shove with the paddle tip off the bank or beach. While on quiet water, you and your partner should practice going in reverse, just by using the nonpower face of your canoe paddle. Your paddle positions for back paddling (something you may use later for getting around river bends) will be the same as in the forward power stroke, but you will be like a movie in reverse. Your strokes will also be shorter.

It will be a simple matter for both of you to propel the boat backward for a few yards, but it takes real teamwork to accomplish a straight line or turns in both directions. For serious white-water paddlers and slalom racers, mastery is essential. I could fill the next few pages with diagrams, but they would be more confusing than constructive. It's something you should experiment with, especially if you think you're headed for the world of white water.

The solo paddler, sitting on the bow seat, facing the stern, or kneeling in front of the center thwart, can manage all the necessary turns and maneuvers described for tandem paddlers with J stroke, stern pry, and stern sweep, observing earlier admonitions about windvaning, should a breeze come up.

Running the Fond du Lac.

# 5

# Skills for Moving Water

The same canoe that can be totally forgiving on a small lake under gentle breezes can become a stubborn or frisky critter when waters begin to move. A familiar story is the novice canoer who heads off down the lake with a nice tail wind and, if able to turn around at all, finds that the two miles covered in forty-five minutes by coasting downwind now entail two hours of head-down digging, which neither the novice's muscles nor skills are up to. If breezes are stiff or gusting, paddlers just trying to come about are going to have a struggle on their hands, particularly if they are light in the bow.

Wind is the canoeist's most frustrating adversary. There is only one technique for dealing with heavy winds and white-capped waters: Avoid them! Until you know the limits of your ability, err on the side of conservatism. A canoe weighing 70 pounds and presenting a broad surface is highly vulnerable to the wind. At best, strong breezes will hamper your forward progress; at worst, they can raise seas sufficient to swamp your boat or commit you to a course not of your choosing.

Avoidance does not mean total abstinence; a strategy designed to minimize the effects of wind should be your objective. If you must paddle, stay as close to land as is practical and try to use a lee shore (out of the wind), if available. One learns from experience, however, that on larger bodies of water the wind and its effects tend to conform to the configuration of the lake, so that a west wind can seem to come from three directions at once, making progress difficult for a canoe headed southwest, west, or northwest. In a channel or river that trends to the northwest, a west wind will funnel through the valley created by the channel, so that you in your canoe will perceive it as a northwest wind.

Nonetheless, your strategy will be one of seeking the lee shores and hugging them to minimize the consequences of a swamping. All this may sound ominous, so I hasten to say that in thirty years of canoeing we have never been swamped, nor have any of my acquaintances. But the danger exists, and your awareness and good judgment are the best safeguards.

The greatest danger is the sudden rising of a squall or thunderstorm with canoers committed to the open reaches of a large lake and far from shore. A nose for changing weather is a good ally.

## QUARTERING

The strokes for coping with windy waters are essentially no different from those already described, but positiveness of execution and mastery of paddling a straight line gives you an edge. Obviously, a zigzagging canoe is an inefficient one, requiring extra energy you can ill afford in such circumstances and providing more opportunities for the wind to snatch or shove at your bow.

A kneeling position should be your first tactic. Next comes the orientation of your canoe to the waves, analogous to "tacking" in a sailboat. You need to pick the best line: basically, the route that achieves your objective (a dock, point of land, or lee shore) without putting your broadside to the waves or committing you even further to windy reaches of the lake.

The tactic here is known as "quartering," and whether you are running with or paddling against the wind, your canoe's steerage and stability are improved by moving obliquely to the line of the waves.

The quartering tactic lengthens the peaks and troughs of the waves and tends to lessen the precipitous rise and fall of bow and stern which results from hitting the waves straight on. It's usually the slap into the trough that puts a bucketful of water in the bow paddler's lap.

Running with the wind is also best done at a quartering angle. It is one of the great sensations in canoeing, but it also presents challenges. Depending on your canoe, its load, and your headway, you will get some "surfing" action, but as the following seas build, you will find yourself sliding off the backs of

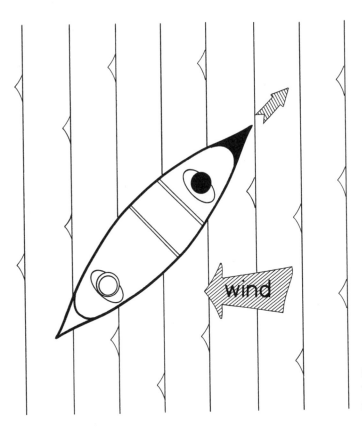

Quartering into the waves is the best way to paddle against the wind.

the waves, your stern sinking into the trough, as the next breaking wave threatens to wash over the gunwales, right at the stern seat.

Your paddle strokes heading into the wind must be deliberate and, for the stern paddler, correcting strokes must be applied forcefully while paying attention to the angle of attack. Here is an instance where you may want to ignore earlier suggestions that you and your partner pick a paddling side and stick with it. Two paddlers quartering into the waves and paddling on their strong sides may well find that a switch to the opposite sides will mean more effective use of the stern pry, the stern's strongest stroke. And yet there are some combinations of wind velocity and direction, wave action, quartering angle, canoe trim, and relative strength of bow and stern paddler that make it easier to paddle just as is, the stern paddler discovering that a pry or rudder need be applied only occasionally, with a stern sweep added every now and then to keep the canoe from veering broadside into the trough.

Running both against and with the wind, there is some danger of spinning on the top of a wave, so the bow and stern paddlers may want to use their pry

A                                                            B

*Stern Pry and Bow Cross Draw*
Together, the stern pry and bow cross drawn turn the canoe here sharply to the right (A,B). In C, the bow paddler from his normal paddling position, without changing his grip, swings his paddle across the bow and plants it well out from the opposite side of the canoe.

and draw, respectively, as bracing or outrigging. One or the other paddler must have firm purchase on some piece of water. In the stern, you can convert your stern pry into a brace by moving the heel of your hand (in the prying sequence) back, or off the gunwale, twisting the paddle blade with your lower hand to put the nonpower face flat on the water, and putting your weight on it. You have just created an outrigger.

The bow paddler likewise may use the draw stroke, not as a means of turning the canoe but of also creating an outrigger. In white water these techniques will be refined and carried further.

## THE CROSS DRAW

We will cover white-water techniques in chapter 7, but there are many little streams, offering delightful canoeing, whose tight bends can be as challenging as a slalom course. A moderate current compounds the challenge. Anticipation

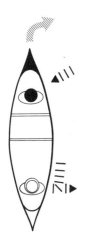

C

—making your moves before you are too far into the bend—will put you mostly in control. More than a few experienced canoers have ended up tangled in the alders on the outside of a tight little bend, so be prepared to take a few of those turns with good humor.

The stern pry is your staple, and for tight turns to your off side it's time to break the rules again: Switch paddling sides and pry away. In these situations the person in the bow really works and should, in fact, be the one to anticipate and initiate the appropriate moves, which includes watching out for the inevitable snags that are a part of little-river canoeing. The bow paddler's draw stroke must be sharper and more anticipatory, and a new stroke, the cross draw, must be mastered.

The bow paddler does not change grips for this stroke, but turns the entire upper body and shoulders toward the off-paddling (opposite) side, swinging the paddle up and over the bow, the elbow of the upper paddling arm tucked into the side. The bow paddler then extends the lower arm and trunk to plant the blade well out from the canoe. As with the draw, the end of the canoe is pulled to the paddle and the blade is quickly raised from the water before it goes under the boat.

So much for the little streams. They're fun, and every bend can bring a fresh surprise. Remember that the current is fastest at the outside of a bend, and that there are plenty of opportunities to get in a jam. So make sure you have your strokes down pat on flat water.

## THE BOW PRY

Most of the important interchangeable strokes have been discussed, such as stern sweep and stern draw and stern pry and reverse sweep. Now let's look at an alternative to the cross draw, the bow pry. You may want to experiment with it, since some people find it a little tricky, particularly in fast-moving or heavy water, but it is effective!

There should be some forward momentum of the canoe; then you push the blade straight down into the water, on a plane with the keel line and well ahead of the bow seat. Just as with the stern pry, you may use the gunwale as a fulcrum. Actually, if the boat has sufficient momentum, and especially in fast-moving water, just holding the blade perpendicular while leaning *away* (downstream, if you're on a river) will move your bow over smartly.

## PADDLING RIVERS WITH GRADIENT

Gradient is simply the total feet of altitude drop of a river, or the section to be run, divided by the number of miles under consideration. Thus a river that drops 100 feet in 100 miles has a one-foot-per-mile gradient, which translates into a very moderate current. Assuming the gradient is constant, a one-to-four-foot gradient per mile would, in all likelihood, have very little white water. You had better be certain that the gradient applies to the river section you are running, however. The Fond du Lac River in northern Saskatchewan has only a two-foot drop per mile over its 250-mile distance, but there are lake expansions of oceanlike proportions along its route, so that most of the drop takes place in narrower sections of the river, where roaring cataracts and incredible waterfalls render these sections unrunnable.

To develop new skills, consider low-gradient rivers but ones with a good solid current, perhaps 4 to 8 mph. The Yukon, for example, would run in the upper part of that range. Such rivers are also known as Class I, defined by the International Scale of River Difficulty as "moving water with a few riffles and small waves. Few or no obstructions." (See chapter 8 for the complete classification.)

Your principal concern on such rivers will be sand or gravel bars and "sweepers"—obstacles such as brush or fallen trees that allow the current through but can trap your canoe. As you have learned from the little rivers, the current is fastest toward the outside of a bend. Often this is where the sweepers lodge, reaching far out into the water and representing an obstacle—indeed, a danger —to the canoer. By positioning yourself well before you get into the turn, and letting the current work for you, you can negotiate the big bends easily. The specific technique is known as the "back ferry," or setting around a bend.

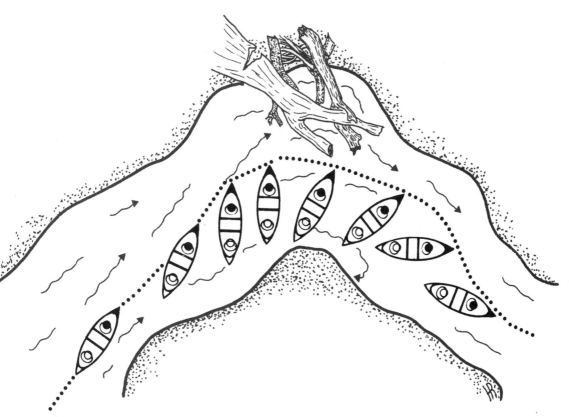

Back ferry: setting around a bend.

In the back ferry, the canoe doesn't make its turn until well into the bend, since you hold the canoe in a position relative to the direction of the current rather than to the shore. By putting your canoe into reverse, back paddling, you can keep to the inside of the bend until you are much of the way through; the naturally faster current coming from the outside of the bend gives the bow of the canoe a shove in the right direction. This is a maneuver that can only be learned on the water, and the speed of the current and configuration of the river will dictate your angle of attack and the force of your back paddle. It is also worth knowing what *not* to do: Don't paddle with a full head of steam into the bend and become overcommitted to the outside before it's too late. You want to have your boat moving slower than the current as you make the turn.

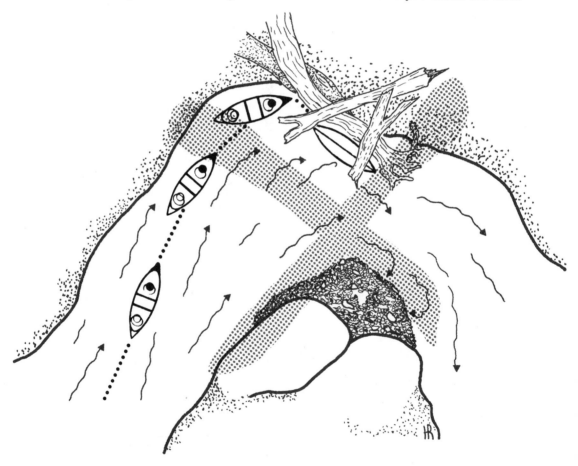

Danger of canoe becoming overcommitted to outside of bend.

## Other Ways Around

If you and your partner are not yet a well-oiled machine capable of coordinating both the strength of the back paddle and the correct angle of the canoe—or if the inside of the bend is filled by a gravel bar—you may find the back ferry is impractical. Often the gravel bar forces you into a narrow channel and toward the outside of the bend. In this case, you may enter the top of the channel with your bow well angled toward the inside of the bend. At times, and depending on the speed of the river or the steepness of the gradient, you may be almost broadside to the current, attempting to ride the inside edge of the main current (specifically, the eddy line described in chapter 6) and straightening out the canoe as soon as the obstacle is passed.

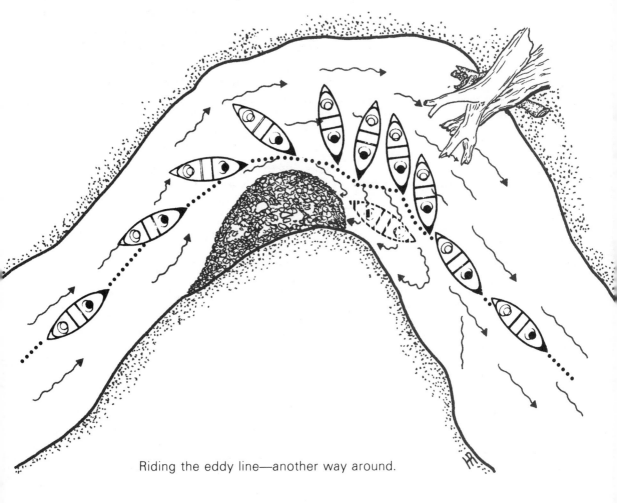

Riding the eddy line—another way around.

If the outside of the bend contains an unnerving entanglement of logs or debris, or if the currents are persuasively strong and you want to play it conservatively, there is still another ploy: Not only do you bring your canoe broadside as you move down the channel, you get your bow pointed upstream and cross over the eddy line into the backwater below the bar on the inside of the bend. If you should cross the eddy line before your bow is angled upstream, be prepared to lean to the inside of your turn. The technique, known as eddying in, is described in greater detail in chapter 6.

## THE UPSTREAM FERRY

Another maneuver, and one which helps explain the principles involved in the back ferry (although not designed to get you around river bends), is the upstream ferry. This has two main purposes on a fast-moving river: one is to permit you to hit a shoreline target as you move downriver; the other is to get you from one side of the river to the other—that is, directly across—without being swept far downstream. The principle used is the same as that of the

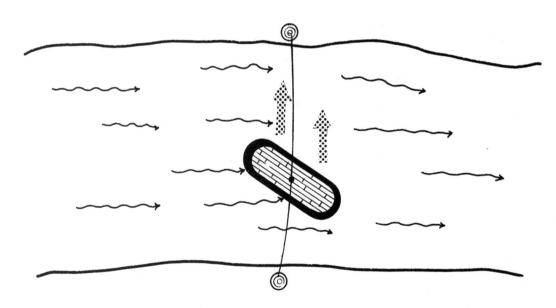

The ferryboat illustrates the principle of the upstream ferry.

oldtime ferry, which had only river current as its motive power. Tethered to a stationary cable stretched across the river, the ferry moved directly across under the cable by being angled right or left, according to the direction of the onrushing river current.

Instead of the cable and tether, the paddlers of a canoe must provide sufficient headway to maintain the angle which will allow the river current to move the canoe straight across. It's the angle that's important; if you have to paddle too hard, your angle is wrong. In general, the stronger the current, the more acute the angle.

The upstream ferry is probably the most useful tactic in all river canoeing. It should be practiced at every opportunity and mastered before any rivers of consequence are attempted. While there is much Class I water that can be enjoyed without this tool, it is a must for white water of all grades, and a technique you will want to take on any canoe trip involving large rivers with gradient.

# An Introduction to Fast Water

Learning to read rivers is an important skill for any canoeist, whether you are planning to tackle white water or not. This chapter will discuss faster water in general and then describe skills necessary for running it.

## WATER VOLUME

Class II water, according to the International Scale of River Difficulty, contains "easy rapids with waves up to three feet, and wide clear channels that are obvious without scouting. Some maneuvering is required." Class III water has "rapids with high irregular waves often capable of swamping an open canoe, and narrow passages that often require complex maneuvering. Many require scouting from shore." In general, Class III water is only suitable for open canoes at lower water levels. Class III should be considered the upper limit of navigability for canoes unless they have decking of some sort and additional flotation.

The classification of a river is a function of its gradient and of obstacles such as boulders, ledges, and narrow chutes. These indigenous features tell us the river's potential, but it is the volume of

89

water that creates the reality. One so-called Class II river, when swollen by rains or spring runoff, can become precarious for an open canoe; another Class II river with different features may well flatten out at high-water levels, as rocks and ledges are covered, and paddlers here can look forward to a big, fast, yet relatively safe ride.

## Handling High Water

While different riverbed configurations will react differently to high volumes of water flow, it is best to start off by assuming that high water will increase a river's degree of difficulty. Never underestimate the power of moving water. Its force appears to increase geometrically as volume increases; thus, the strength and swiftness of stroke execution must likewise be increased. The consequences of a capsize in high water can be severe, as canoers struggle against a powerful current and their swamped canoe, weighing the equivalent of two tons of hydraulic force, lumbers downstream. Although obstacles are fewer in high water, the reaction time to avoid those remaining is greatly shortened, and the associated turbulence is substantially increased.

## Handling Low Water

Low water levels, on the other hand, bring their own special problems. Boulders and ledges that were covered by higher water are now revealed in profusion; maneuvering becomes more complex. However, you will have more time to react, since your canoe is not moving as fast, and the consequences of a dump are not as severe. Currents, eddies, and standing waves—soon to be discussed —are more benign and forgiving of poor technique.

## KNOW YOUR RIVER

Local reports provided by knowledgeable people are your best guide to classification. Knowledgeable people are those who recognize *your* skill level and who have run the river recently in a boat similar to yours. People who live on the river are likely to be unreliable too, unless they are canoers; they can be either too optimistic about a river's navigability or overly conservative. Ready to start down a sizable river in Quebec, our crew sought out an Indian who had lived along its banks all his life. His ominous description of the river and its perilous course would have caused any sane person to abandon the expedition forthwith. Once under way, however, we relied on our own scouting and judgment. The river was challenging, but hardly unrunnable.

If rapids on a river generally fit into one of the following classifications, but the water temperature is below 50°F, or if the trip is an extended one into wilderness area, the river should be considered one class more difficult than normal.

**CLASS I** Moving water with a few rifles and small waves. Few or no obstructions.

**CLASS II** Easy rapids with waves up to 3 feet and wide, clear, channels that are obvious without scouting. Some maneuvering is required.

**CLASS III** Rapids with high, irregular waves often capable of swamping an open canoe. Narrow passages that often require complex maneuvering. May require scouting from shore.

**CLASS IV** Long, difficult rapids with constricted passages that often require precise maneuvering in very turbulent waters. Scouting from shore is necessary, and conditions make rescue difficult. *Generally not possible for open canoes*. Boaters in covered canoes and kayaks should have the ability to Eskimo roll.

**CLASS V** Extremely difficult, long, and very violent rapids with highly congested routes, which always should be scouted from shore. Rescue conditions are difficult, and there is significant hazard to life in the event of a mishap. Ability to Eskimo roll is essential for boaters in kayaks and decked canoes.

**CLASS VI** Difficulties of Class V carried to the extreme of navigability. Nearly impossible and very dangerous. For teams of experts only, after close study has been made and all precautions have been taken.

UNSUITABLE FOR OPEN CANOES

Being able to read water is a prerequisite to running rapids.

River guidebooks, if they have been conscientiously written by someone who has run the river within the last five years, can be a helpful starting point. Next, check with a member of a local canoe club who has either run the river recently or has information from someone who has. Remember, though, that much misinformation is dispensed, and reports that are valid are often ignored by would-be canoeists. On crowded waters, if air and water temperatures are warm and potential rescuers numerous, the novices who are over their heads —actually and figuratively—can be fished out. With increasing frequency, unfortunately, the consequences can be tragic, as more and more canoers with no knowledge of either canoeing basics or safety precautions tackle strange rivers. Know the water you are running, and take with you the requisite skills.

## READING WATER

Most Class II water can be run by competent paddlers without scouting—if your information is accurate! Most Class III water, on the other hand, probably requires scouting before running, unless you are following a competent leader who knows the river. Scouting a section of river determines the best route around or through a series of obstacles—or if the section should be run at all. A downed tree from a recent storm, an unrunnable ledge exposed by lower-than-normal water, or dangerously high standing waves created by high water may lead to a decision to carry around a particular stretch.

What exactly are you looking for? If one were to conduct a controlled laboratory experiment, whereby a flow of water was directed with even velocity down a perfectly straight line, etched in a solid but yielding bed such as clay, one would discover after some period of time that the "river" would begin to oscillate, or meander, rhythmically. Of course, real rivers do not descend absolutely uniform gradients through uniform mediums. In addition to clay of varying density, there are gravels, loose soil, formations of sandstone and shale, and obstacles created by intrusive geologic formations. All these features give the river its character, but it is the river's tendency to oscillate, all else being equal, that governs its existence.

As you spend more time on a river, you become increasingly aware of how its main current moves back and forth; first left, undercutting the bank; then seeming to bounce off in the opposite direction; then sweeping in a new arc into the right bank. As you come to recognize the rhythm of river currents, their anomalies, and their interruptions and irregularities, the apparent contradictions become more understandable.

Haystacks are standing waves created by the collision of fast water with the slower water at the bottom of a drop.

## Haystacks

Generally speaking, the current will be faster at the center of the river in straight sections and slower near the banks. Yet as you approach a bend, the faster current runs to the outside of the bend. For most Class II water—almost by definition—the main current will be the best route. The absence of "white" water is not the determinant of the best channel; indeed, the standing waves created by the constriction of the main river current between obstacles, or by a narrowing of the riverbanks, is just the place to be. As long as these standing waves, or haystacks, created by the collision of the faster-moving waters of the main current with the slower waters at the bottom of the drop, are not of a magnitude to bury the bow of the canoe, it is better to put a few ladlefuls of water in the bow paddler's lap than to opt for the gravel bars or ledges at the sides.

## Finding the Channel

Viewed from above, the inside of the bend may appear inviting in the absence of the unnerving splash of white water, but as canoers bear down on this "safer" channel, they may discover that there is insufficient water to get a canoe through, and the white that was not to be seen from above is now frothing at the base of a foot-and-a-half-high ledge. High water levels, on the other hand, may call for running the inside of the bend.

Often, you will be looking for a channel within a channel, but the principles are the same. If you look at the accompanying diagram you can visualize the "V," or tongue of water, which is created by a breach in an obstruction or by the force of water as it is constricted by two immovable obstacles.

These paddlers head for the V or tongue of water between two obstructions. (Below) The V.

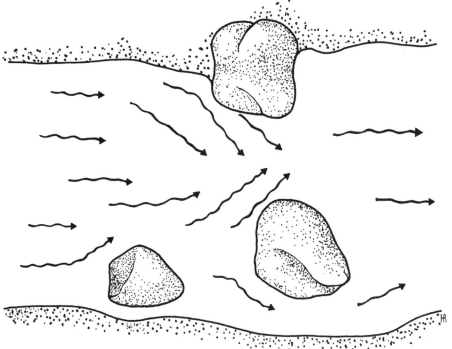

# The Class III Rapid

If we add a few more obstructions to the diagram, we can create a Class III rapid, which by definition requires scouting and complex maneuvering. Additional geologic irregularities have interrupted the course and gradient of the river, so that the route is now in doubt. If gradient or water volume is increased, so is the degree of difficulty. A greater number of obstacles, or constrictions, cause the water to quicken or surge.

This new set of conditions calls for careful scouting. You should look for possible traps as well as escapes. You need to know where to go, how to get there, and what to do when you do get there; if you have any serious doubts, you shouldn't be there at all. Time to carry.

Class III water does have a route; it's just hard to find. The need to avoid rocks and boulders is obvious, but finding the inviting tongue (or "V") between two rocks, only to find a house-size boulder waiting at the bottom, can be discouraging. That's one trap. The other is the holes created by submerged boulders or ledges.

It is not the hole itself that is a problem; many small holes can be blasted through with hardly a bobble. The ones to be reckoned with are usually filled with foam that is more air than water and incapable of supporting the weight of boat and paddlers. The first casualty, as usual, is the bow paddler, who is buried as the diving bow keeps on diving. If the hole is not too large, and the paddlers can coordinate their braces and strong power strokes to pull themselves out of the hole, they may be only held up for a split second, take in a little water over the gunwales, and continue on. A more serious hole can eat a boat, holding it indefinitely and violently ejecting the paddlers from their craft.

# Eddies

Needless to say, if there is any question about a set of rapids, avoid them. Aside from paddling techniques necessary for negotiating complex rapids, there are some escape hatches known as *eddies*.

You will find that behind each major obstruction or sharp corner there is a circulating current. That is the eddy current, and it is going upstream against the main current. Depending on the vigor of this circulation relative to the main downstream current, the eddy can be both a trap and an escape, but we'll discuss that in more detail later. For the time being, consider an eddy as a haven, a place to pull into for a rest while you scout the rest of the drop or reorganize your strategy.

# RUNNING A CLASS III RAPID

Take the bow position in my canoe, and we will try to negotiate a complex section of water employing some of the strokes we have already learned on quieter waters, adding a few new techniques and strokes, dodging the traps and using the eddies. At first the channel is obvious as we follow the smooth tongue of water inclining downhill with deceptive smoothness. Then the narrowing of the channel and the ultimate collision with the quieter waters below combine to throw up a crosshatching of haystacks. We'll get a little wet but the channel is "clean," and our only strategy will be to stay mostly in line with the main force of the current and, if the waves are particularly heavy, to slow our momentum to minimize the rise and fall of our bow.

## Standing Waves

As we near the bottom of the drop, we find that standing waves are piling up, creating higher peaks and deeper troughs. You have already learned the bracing stroke on the lake rollers, and you rotate your shoulders toward the gunwale, punching out with your lower hand—your paddle blade at a slight climbing angle to the water—and leaning on this stabilizing outrigger. As the canoe tops the crest of the next wave, threatening to spin us broadside, I quickly rotate my shoulders toward the water, reaching out with my paddle blade to catch a piece of the retreating wave. In fact, if I twist my torso far enough around and increase the angle of paddle bite, I can actually slow the canoe while maintaining stability.

As we reach the final climax of the drop, you decide that you're tired of taking water into your lap, and to slow the boat and minimize the slap into the final wave trough, you simply jam the paddle blade vertically into the water, prying up and forward and literally letting the boat down. We rest below, exhilarated by our rollercoaster ride and only a little wet.

## Scouting from an Eddy

We now approach a bend to the right, but a house-sized boulder stands to the left of center just at the start of the bend, and the sharpness of the turn itself suggests that we need to stop and look the situation over. Just to our left is a low but unrunnable ledge, and just below that a protruding rock with a hole behind it. The main current is unmistakably to the far right, but we will not commit ourselves to the river before we have done some scouting.

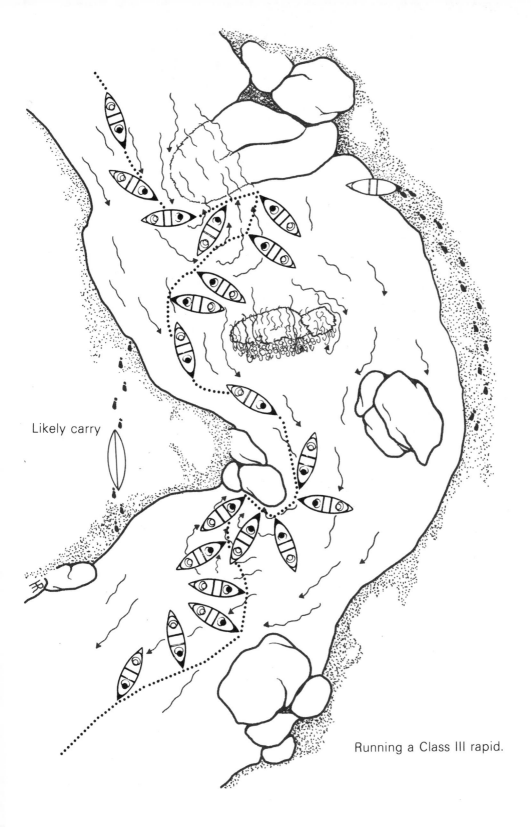

Likely carry

Running a Class III rapid.

Just behind the ledge on our left is a gently swirling eddy. Barely grazing the ledge with our left gunwale, we drive the bow of the canoe into its embrace. To do this, you start a draw stroke from your left-sided paddling position, making sure that you have crossed the eddy line and that you are planting your paddle into the eddy current, not the downstream current. You both draw and brace, putting your weight on the paddle blade and leaning hard to the inside of the turn. I am giving a hard sweep in the stern and leaning to the inside of the turn as well—but only after we cross the eddy line. The opposing direction of eddy and main current grab bow and stern respectively, actually whipping the boat around to face upstream. Since the bow draw is a power stroke—compared to my sweep and somewhat awkward lean to the side opposite my paddling side—you are in control for our eddy-in to the left.

Our reconnaissance reveals a clean channel to the far right, but we must be wary of being swept across and into the outside of the bend, where the water is piling up, to collide a little farther down with an unfriendly boulder. The river level is moderate to low, and we feel strong and confident.

## Leaving the Eddy and Upstream Ferry

First we must extricate ourselves from the eddy and execute a short upstream ferry, to get ourselves across and above the rock and hole blocking the center of the channel. Below our first ledge, we are looking upstream, and now, with positive forward strokes, we drive the bow of the canoe across the eddy line and, maintaining a fine angle toward the opposite shore, allow the current to "ferry" us across. As soon as we have cleared the offending boulder and hole, you lean downstream, positively, and draw. Also leaning downstream, I sweep on the right as we come full around to point downriver. Oriented to the main body of the current, we both backpaddle slightly to slow ourselves and prepare for the next crucial move.

## Eddying In

Just behind the jutting point which fills the inside of the bend is a boiling eddy. It will not be quite so forgiving of technique as our first one, so our strokes must be more precise and our lean, as we drop into the eddy, more positive. We have practiced our draws—including the cross draw—on calm water, and gone so far as to practice using a gently sloping shore or riverbank to get the feel of really leaning on our paddle. We found that by using hips, knees, and paddle we could heel the boat right over to the gunwale and bring it back up. Moving away from shore, we discovered that with our paddle blade properly angled we could perform the same maneuver using the water.

A

Б

C

*Entering an Eddy*
Paddlers drive across the eddy line into the eddy created by the boulder in the foreground (A). Using a stern sweep and bow draw (or high brace), both A and B show them leaning into the turn: they lost it momentarily in C and steady in D.

D

E

D

No time for reminiscing now! You rotate your torso fully from left to right, your upper elbow in tight against your ribs. Don't make a stroke; just get that blade into the water of the eddy immediately behind the point and lean on it as I pry hard on my right stern and lean hard to the right. The swirling currents of the eddy stop the canoe dead, but the rush of the river past the point punches the stern around. We are saved from being capsized only by our strong lean to the inside of the turn as we eddy in. So violent is our pivot that I must catch the careening stern with a low brace. Laying the nonpower face of the blade well out—and flat—on the water, I create a platform.

## Eddying Out

We've made it. We give each other an encouraging word, compliment ourselves on a job well done. But our biggest challenge lies immediately ahead. With what is popularly known as a "peel-out," we must now get ourselves back across that violent eddy line, created by a powerful downstream current and its abrupt interruption by the point behind which we now rest—subdued but anticipating. By backing downstream somewhat, we can attack the eddy line a little farther down, where the demarcation is not so severe.

This upstream ferry starts as the paddlers drive their canoe across the eddy line into the main current (A). A strong pry (B, C) in the stern maintains the angle as the downstream current pushes the canoe across the river (C,D,E).

C

B

A

Getting into an eddy in heavy rapids requires more positive bracing and leaning into the turn. Note how far the bow paddler is out over the water.

Ready, we drive the bow out of the eddy. You hesitate for just a moment in the bow; your downstream lean and switch from left to right side for the cross draw is timorous—indecisive—like the downhill skier who instinctively leans toward the false security of the hill when the steep is suddenly intimidating. I try to compensate, but it is too late. In a twinkling, the downrushing current has pulled our upstream gunwale under, and we are going for a swim. Fortunately, the river empties into a quiet pool below, where we are able to quickly get ourselves and the boat to shore—our egos the only casualty.

Getting out of a strong eddy is one of the most difficult maneuvers in white-water canoeing, and for one of the partners there is an awkward lean downstream that must be made to the off side. When the off side happens to be the bow paddler's—as with our episode—the fact of the bow's being the first to face the torrent is even more critical. Only practice, and even getting wet, ultimately gives you the technique and the confidence to master the peel-out. The route to mastery is to practice these movements at every opportunity in modest eddies, exaggerating your execution and leans and working up a progression of difficulty.

Another way to eddy in. The stern paddler is lying on a low brace, leaning to the inside of the turn. The bow is using a bow pry as an alternate to the bow cross draw.

These paddlers are "peeling out" of an eddy, using a stern sweep and bow draw and high brace. Note their exaggerated lean downstream as they hit the main current and hold it until they are pointed straight downriver.

## Role of the Bow Paddler

It's appropriate to comment here that the bow paddler's role in white water is crucial, and when the waters begin to rumble, the partner in the bow should become the captain. The bow is a better vantage point for reading the water, and the split-second advantage in decision making may be the difference between success and disaster. It is not unusual to see the stronger male partner in the bow, even among experienced male-female and husband-wife paddling teams, and including international competition. One enterprising instructor, who has given white-water clinics for years on the upper Hudson River, first puts the paddlers, many of whom are family members, into covered single canoes so that everyone learns both bow and stern strokes. It's a great idea.

The skills described up to this point will more than adequately equip you for both modest and ambitious adventures. Mastery of the strokes, and the gradual learning of the ways of moving waters, whether found on lakes or in the river valleys, should give you the confidence to tackle the sport of white water (described in the next chapter), canoe trips and the expeditions that grip your imagination.

## LINING

There are times when a ledge or severe drop or a too-shallow riffle makes paddling dangerous or impractical. This is more of a problem for the canoe

tripper who does not want to unload the canoe and make a portage (lining is described in more detail in chapter 9), but you may have occasion to line whenever you face such obstacles on a river.

By means of sturdy lines attached to bow and stern, the canoeing partners can alternately guide and restrain the canoe down and around offending obstacles. This can be managed from shore, but often requires the canoers to do some wading.

Canoe instruction is available and fun.

# 7

# The World of White Water

There are thousands of canoers who will never taste white water, nor have they the slightest inclination to do so. Indeed, you can enjoy an extraordinary variety of canoeing experiences, including ambitious and remote canoe trips, without ever tackling more than Class II waters; when you venture beyond well-traveled waterways, all questionable rapids should be portaged anyway.

This chapter deals with white water not as some obstacle encountered while canoeing but as a sport in itself. The fanaticism of those who follow the rivers is akin to the surfer's quest for the ninth wave. The rush of adrenaline that even veteran paddlers experience as they hear the first roar of a boulder-choked drop and see the horizon line sink ominously is something to be experienced. The line of trees noticeably below those surrounding you, the spray dancing at the lip of the abyss, the smell of mist—all send signals to the brain and you are instantly on guard, tingling and alert. There is nothing like it.

The white-water buff is endlessly fascinated by the crescendos created by moving water. You have, yourself, probably stood and stared with awe at a plunging waterfall. True white-water fanatics will stop and look at—and analyze ex-

White-water requires finely honed reflexes. This downstream lean is too late, with the result that the paddler is being pulled into a hole.

haustively—almost anything that moves. After they have run a drop, cleanly or ignominiously, the chute, wave, hole, or eddy will be examined again, admired, or cursed, as it changes before the eye. Should the wave or hole be blessed with particular dynamics, perhaps discernible only to the eyes of the cultist, he or she will return again and again and again, to surf or perchance to perform the incredible and elusive "ender" or tip stand; this is the white-water freak's nirvana.

White-water canoeing may be an end in itself, but it can also be the only means to explore an unspoiled canyon or experience solitude in a shrinking wilderness. For a few hours the sounds of water racing over rocks remove the river runner from the world of freeways and civilized bustle.

## BOATS AND EQUIPMENT

The sport of white-water canoeing—and its sister sport, kayaking—continues to grow as canoers who have been actively paddling flat water, have perhaps tasted Class I and II rivers, or have taken canoe trips which prudently bypassed many sets of rapids start to think about converting their 17-foot Grumman aluminums to white-water boats. Only the best canoeists should consider this.

Canoeing parties should include no fewer than three canoes, paddlers should have had previous experience or instruction in white water, and at least one in the party should have firsthand knowledge of the river to be run.

### Open Boats

Actually, most good recreational canoes (those within the parameters of the table in chapter 1) can be made suitable for white water if their design makes sense; they should be deep and full-bowed boats, with at least a moderate rocker and a minimum of keel. Extra flotation, such as ethafoam blocks, inner tubes, or the air bags specifically designed for white water, is essential. A swamped canoe in a fast-moving river is a dangerous beast among rocks and boulders. It is extraordinarily difficult to recover if it gets away from you and into the next drop.

Class III water at moderate or high-water levels, and Class IV water at any level, calls for full decking, usually a coated nylon or Dacron cover. The picture shows one homemade design employing snaps, but there are commercially available full-length decks as well.

Your paddles can be those you use in flat water, but many white-water

(Left) Thigh braces and knee pads provide better control to the white-water paddler. (Below) Full-length decking for an open canoe may be necessary for heavy white-water or expedition canoeing.

paddlers prefer slightly shorter ones. A T grip, slightly oval shaft, and sturdy blade with tip protection are also favored. Since you'll be kneeling most of the time, you should install some foam or neoprene knee pads, using epoxy or contact cement. Serious white-water buffs will probably want to install thigh braces or straps. These give very positive control and enable you to get well out over the water.

A good bow and stern line should be accessible for rescue but secured out of the way. A sponge and a bailer fashioned out of an old bleach bottle make up the rest of your white-water open-canoe accouterments. A helmet is advisable, and, if water temperatures are in the sixties or below, a wet suit is a must.

## Closed Boats

Remember that the negotiating of Class III or IV water by an open canoe, regardless of extra flotation or full decking, is for expert canoeists only. These waters are really the province of a very special kind of boat: the C-1 and C-2. Closely related to the kayak, both in appearance and performance, the C-1 and C-2 (C for canoe; 1 or 2 for single or double place, or port) can negotiate waters of unbelievable ferocity. Only a knowledgeable eye would be able to pick a C-1 out of a crowd of kayaks (often abbreviated as K-1's). But they are very different boats. The C-1 paddler, rather than sitting and employing a double-bladed paddle, kneels and uses a single-bladed canoe paddle. Because kneeling puts the canoer's center of gravity higher than the kayaker's, the C-1 is a larger-volume boat and usually wider at the midsection. Whereas the kayaker sits and is braced at the feet, with knees against the upper deck, the canoer kneels, with the buttocks on a saddle, thwart, or pillar, and establishes "oneness" with the canoe by means of thigh straps. (The straps that are optional in an open canoe are a necessity in the C-1.)

Thus secured, the C-1 paddler can execute an amazing array of powerful strokes, including the "Eskimo roll" normally associated with kayaks. But the C-1 and its strokes are difficult to master, and most kayakers are appalled at the tortures associated with prolonged kneeling and the absence of a second paddle blade.

The C-1 paddler must master the off-side problem without a partner. Nevertheless, the C-1'er sings the praises of this boat. The higher angle of vision permits more effective reading of the water and, because of the higher position, more powerful leverage. Also, if you have been a canoer all your life—meaning you probably started out paddling open canoes—you're already one-sided and like the familiar feel of kneeling to use a single-bladed paddle.

The C-1 paddler's accessories include PFD, helmet, spray skirt, paddle jacket, wet suit, and booties. Note spare paddle holder and rear grab line for safety.

A slalom C-2 is the two-man craft for racing or heavy white-water cruising.

In world competition, where Europeans have long dominated the white-water sports, recent years have seen Americans competing and winning in the C-1 and C-2 classes. Many viewers of the televised Munich Olympics in 1972 thought they were watching an American kayaker take a silver medal. He was, in fact, paddling a C-1. More recently, some of the C-1's from the Washington, D.C., canoe club have been beating the times of the K-1's on the same slalom course, a fit coming-of-age for the boat with truly North American roots.

Both C-1's and C-2's come in a wide range of designs and purposes, usually in fiberglass and Kevlar, but with the exception of a few large C-2 designs, most of these boats are designed for very quick turning. The touring boats, so-called, have a greater volume and can negotiate very heavy water with remarkable aplomb. Increasingly, however, white-water boaters are favoring lower-volume low-profile boats. These require greater paddling skill but they play the surfing waves and holes like a ballet dancer and sneak the slalom gates like the smaller-volume kayaks. In fact, the more extreme slalom designers have developed lines that would have been considered radical for *kayaks* a few years ago.

The C-1 is almost strictly a high-powered white-water boat, generally unsuitable for any extended touring. However, there are several C-2 designs that could be of interest to the canoer who is considering longer trips, involving extensive rapids, or who would like to get into closed boating without going to one of the temperamental slalom designs. These boats can carry two weeks' gear or more. Even for weekend jaunts, if your partner is less skilled, the stability and security of a big-volume closed boat is attractive.

## GETTING STARTED

If you live near white water, and if farther horizons beckon, learn to paddle a C-1 or C-2. Even if canoe tripping is your ultimate objective, the skills that can be gained in working with the C-1 are invaluable. To understand and master the C-1 is to learn as much as can be learned about the white-water paddling sport and the dynamic uses of paddle, body, and boat. At the very least, a C-1 paddler will return to an open canoe with confidence in a higher level of skills and new understanding of the potentials of canoeing.

There are a number of commercial enterprises that offer instruction in C-1, perhaps the best known being John Berry in Riparius, New York, who also builds some remarkable boats and is the original designer of the big C-2 now sold under the name of Berrigan by Old Town. John seems to have pioneered the idea of teaching C-1 technique to paddlers aiming for two-place open boats. Since many of his clients are mixed couples, this breaks with the tradition of the male taking charge of the stern seat and forever relegating wife or companion to motive power in the bow. John teaches women the stern position too, which makes it possible for either parent of a canoe-tripping family to captain a canoe.

Because the C-1 is still a curiosity compared to the kayak, the usual way to get started in white-water boating is through a canoe club—more likely, a kayak and canoe club. In addition to having members with whom you can discuss the sport, clubs generally offer training clinics and winter pool practices. With luck you can find a friendly zealot to lend you a boat and give you a few pointers. (This is definitely a sport to learn in a pool or warm water, since getting wet is as inevitable as the sunrise.)

Having learned the strokes and techniques under controlled conditions and acquired your own C-1, you can tackle, first, Class I and then increasingly more difficult water. Many club outings are designated as training trips in the trip schedule. Seek out rivers that are within your level of ability, and solicit the help of fellow paddlers of greater experience. What you don't want to do is sign up for a Class III trip after three pool sessions and then risk not only your own neck but those of your tripmates as they chase you, your boat, and your paddle downriver all day. The other unpardonable sin is to show up without proper helmet, life vest (PFD), or wet suit (if the water temperature or the season calls for it).

## SKILLS FOR HEAVY WHITE WATER

This does not aim to be a complete text on canoeing heavy white water, either in boats adapted for it by means of extra floatation and decking or in those designed for it, such as C-1's and C-2's. Rather, my intention is to convey something of the excitement of this branch of the sport. The potential canoe tripper or expeditioner should also learn the skills for heavy white water.

### Knowing Where You're At

All strokes described in the preceding chapters are applicable. But inasmuch as the water itself is providing most of your momentum, you will be more concerned with the bracing strokes described later in this chapter. and with an acute awareness of "where you're at." In the heavy white-water environment, fast reaction times are as important as the correctness of the actions themselves. The slightly awkward paddle angle, insincere downstream lean, or momentary delay in execution which was forgiven on Class II water, in a commodious open canoe, will ensure the novice C-1 paddler of a dunking every time.

As "Keep forward in your boots" is the ski instructor's exhortation to the beginning skier, so the novice white-water boater must remember to "lean downstream." The boater's constant challenge is to keep the upstream gunwale away from the river, and to be thinking in terms of always putting the bottom of the boat toward the main force of any current.

## The Wet Exit

As in kayaking, you should first learn the "wet exit," or how to snap off the spray cover and wiggle out of the boat while upside down. Despite the fact that you are tightly cinched in with thigh braces, the wet exit is almost natural, and the purpose of practicing is just so you will not panic when you find yourself upside down on your first river.

## The Eskimo or C-1 Roll

Years ago, the Eskimo roll was thought to be a stunt, capable of being performed by only a virtuoso. Today, it is one of the first things taught to kayakers and canoers. Rolling a C-1 is more difficult than rolling a kayak, although the principle is precisely the same, but as more and more boaters have taken to the sport, the techniques for teaching the roll have advanced apace, so that men, women, and children alike now learn it in several pool sessions.

While full mastery of the roll is not essential—there are some very competent old-time boaters who never learned it—the confidence imparted by having a dependable roll will enable you to pull out more stops in executing every other stroke or maneuver on the river. Temerity and hesitation are the white-water boater's nemesis. Be sure to practice in a controlled environment, such as a pool or warm, shallow lake, so that the inevitable frequent capsizes, followed by righting and emptying the boat, and re-entering and affixing the spray skirt, will not become overly frustrating.

The roll is usually taught after the "wet exit" is mastered. First, get the feel of controlling the boat with your hips and knees and orienting your body to the boat. You can do this best by holding onto the pool side (a dock in the case of a lake) and capsizing toward it. Then twist the boat right side up, keeping your head in the water until the very last and your body close to the boat. You should not be using arms, shoulders, or upper body strength. Concentrate instead on the action of twisting, using hips and knees to roll the canoe upright underneath your more-or-less immobile upper body.

There are four main components to the C-1 roll: the set, the sweep, the paddle-blade flip, and the brace-up. The pictures show the sequence. In the first

A

B

C

*The C-1 Roll*
The paddler sets paddle and blade
(A) and rolls over on paddle side
(B), making sure paddle blade is on
top of water for sweep. In (C) the
sweep has been made, the paddle
blade flipped over, and the paddler braces up, keeping body low
to the deck (D).

D

position the paddle is set. Lean as far forward as possible in your seat and cock the wrist of your lower hand sharply downward. The cocked wrist is to ensure that your blade is on a plane with the surface of the water when you are upside down. (This is crucial for the next step, the sweep.)

Now, roll over in the water toward your paddle side. If you have cocked your wrist hard, as you twist your body the paddle blade should sweep just below the surface of the water—not dive—and draw a great semicircle in the water, from the bow to a point 90 degrees from your cockpit.

Next, quickly turn over the paddle blade. You swept it with the power face down, and it is now flipped onto its nonpower face.

The brace-up is accomplished by pushing downward on the paddle (pushing the nonpower face toward the bottom of the pool) and twisting the hips and torso to turn the boat right side up. This is the motion you learned at the side of the pool. To be successful, you must get the feel of rolling the boat up with your hips, thighs, and knees, concentrating on keeping your head in the water until the boat is almost completely righted.

The learning process is considerably accelerated by having an experienced confederate stand in the pool to orient the paddle blade, guide your sweep, and keep the blade from diving as you brace up. Continue to do this until you get the feel of the movements and become oriented; then see if you can make the moves unaided.

## The Low Brace

As the boat is righted you will be on a low brace, so this is something you may want to practice in advance. Using the pool edge and your hands, you got the feel of righting the boat and keeping your body close to the deck of your boat. Now try it using your paddle blade on the pool edge, tipping the canoe until it is on edge and bringing yourself back up. Or have a buddy stand in the water and hold the paddle blade near the surface of the water. A sloping sandy beach is also a good practice area, if you are learning in a pond or lake.

## The High Brace

When you lean over on the nonpower face of your blade you are in a low brace; on the power face you are in a high brace. Your body and paddle position are just as described for the draw stroke in chapter 4, except that now you are combining it with hip and thigh action to stabilize or right your boat. To be effective, you must really get out over your paddle. Be sure your blade has a slight climbing angle to the water. The wrong angle with your blade will cut

Low brace

The low brace, high brace, and cross draw shown here are basic to staying upright in heavy water.

High brace

Cross draw

a hole in the water, and you will follow it right in. Properly angled, you will find the water just as solid under your paddle as the sand beach you first used for learning.

## The Cross Draw and Brace

Just as the brace is a draw stroke in dynamic suspension, so too the cross draw is used to brace on your off side. It is contorting at first but smooths out with practice. You should practice the cross draw frequently, first as described in chapter 5, as a turning stroke. When adding the brace, the differences will be a more exaggerated twisting of the torso, to get the blade as far away from the boat as possible, and a more positive lean to the off side. In fact, the cross draw and brace is less awkward in moving water (assuming you maintain your nerve and your lean!), where the water does some of the work for you. When you have learned to hold yourself on a cross-draw brace in a surfing wave, you have arrived.

## THE IMPORTANCE OF BRACES

Braces are used as stabilizing and self-recovery tactics and as integral components of the eddy-turning techniques described in chapter 6. A low brace, trailing at a 30-degree angle, could be used to eddy out of a moderately vigorous current, being merely a shift of blade angle after a sharp stern pry to put the bow into the eddy. In leaving a particularly violent chute and entering a powerful eddy, this would be followed by a high brace, making sure that your paddle blade is in the eddy, not in the downstream current. Going into an eddy on your off side is a challenge, but it must be learned as well. It calls for the cross draw described in chapter 5.

It is important to continually practice braces, until the feeling of tipping and popping back up becomes natural and is being done with hip and knee action rather than pure strength. Proficiency in both the high and the low brace will be measured by how far over you can go (including your body completely under water) and still come back up. Braces will be your deliverance in every kind of tough river situation and should become almost automatic. When using either a high or a low brace in a turbulent situation, you will want your upper body bending as low to the deck as you can possibly get it, and your paddle blade well out from the boat. In this attitude, your boat will be laid almost over on its side, with your paddle serving as an outrigger.

In extremely heavy water, braces become more utilized than strokes themselves. The high brace can be locked into and held, or sculled, almost indefinitely as you rollercoaster down a stretch of towering standing waves. It is a powerful brace, and if you find yourself madly careening off the top of a receding wave peak, you can reach back and grab the top of that retreating wave as it passes under you, rather than crash helter-skelter into the waiting trough. But remember that it can be tiring.

The low brace is often used *in extremis* when the paddler, having turned almost fully over on the paddle side, manages to get the nonpower face well extended and rights the canoe, bracing up as described earlier.

Another brace is your forward stroke executed with the body extended well forward from the hips. In fact, any stroke in which you snatch a good piece of water is preferable to doing nothing. A sure sign of a tyro on white water is inaction and rigidity. When heavy waves are encountered, it is the inexperienced or overawed canoeists who either paddle madly in an attempt to gain mastery or freeze in position, putting themselves at the mercy of a superior force. Neither approach makes sense in big water. Canoers who try to power their way through will find themselves out of phase with the rhythm of the river, and at the one moment when a powerful, decisive stroke must be made they may be off balance or spent, or both.

## PLAYING

For paddlers used to the idea of rapids as obstacles, "playing" must seem a strange concept. For the extreme white-water buff, it is an end in itself, and for others of us it is a form of practice, which hones our paddle skills and sharpens our understanding of the infinite contortions of moving water. Playing includes eddy turns, peel-outs, surfing, tip stands, enders, and Lord knows what delights the adventurous can dream up.

When a particularly accommodating combination of water and obstruction is found, the paddler may repeat a maneuver, over and over, such as peeling in and out of the same eddy. Or you may drive your tip upstream into a hole where the opposing forces of the downrushing water on your deck and the curler pushing up under your seat cause the canoe to either attain a state of dynamic equilibrium—hence, "surfing"—or, in a large hole, a tip stand, where the stern will rise at a 90-degree angle to the water. Should you continue end over end, you have completed an "ender," the ultimate hot-dog stunt. Many of these games end in a forced Eskimo roll—or a swim—but only fatigue or boredom will move the paddler downstream to the next playspot, always in search of the perfect wave or the perfect hole.

There are dangers and specific cautions for each of these maneuvers, the holes in particular. The most trouble are holes that turn out to be filled with more foam than water, contain an uncushioned rock, or where the reversal is so powerful that the boater may be held (we call it a "keeper" hole). The ability to recognize a dangerous hole comes only from experience. If your trip leader or an experienced member of the party avoids a particular hole, you had better, too. The practical value of playing, in addition to sharpening your skills, is the tremendous confidence it imparts to the canoer who *inadvertently* gets in a difficult fix. If you have practiced paddling backward down a rapid, for exam-

The paddler is going for a tip stand, playing the water dynamics of the hole.

ple, you will be less likely to panic when, without warning, a rock in midriver spins your canoe around, a not infrequent occurrence. Indeed, a few years ago while canoe tripping on a wild river in British Columbia, my son and I got tangled up and spun around in a shallow labyrinthine drop and were obliged to complete the remaining 75 yards of rapid stern first.

To date, the sport of white-water canoeing (including kayaking) has been a safe one, and the few fatalities that have occurred can be considered freaks. However, as more and more people take up the sport, the chances for serious accidents increase. Highly skilled boaters have taken to running major waterfalls, often having studied the particular hydrostatics or the vertical eddy for days, or even years. Without commenting on the prudence of these endeavors, suffice it to say that there is a danger of latter-day daredevils with lesser credentials getting themselves into fatal situations by attempting to emulate their more talented brethren.

Nevertheless, these are extremes. They in no way diminish the allure of white-water boating as a safe and exciting sport.

# Safety and Fitness

Is canoeing safe? A quick look at statistics is not comforting. Fear of the "tippy" canoe seems to be justified by the numbers of drownings associated with the craft—accidents usually involving hunters, fishermen, or other persons on a spur-of-the-moment canoe adventure. However, while canoes in the hands of the imprudent can be dangerous—like cars or guns—the *sport* of canoeing is safe. Boaters who enjoy canoeing in some organized fashion—canoe tripping, a club affiliation—and have received formal instruction are rarely the victims. As with driving fatalities, alcohol is a frequent accompaniment to canoe drownings, as is ignorance of basic safety practices. Ironically, the fewest fatalities have occurred in the heavy whitewater branch of the sport, presumably because these participants have a healthy respect for the water and have equipped themselves with the necessary skills and protective gear.

## KNOW THE WATER

It is worth repeating that boaters should have accurate foreknowledge of the waters they will be paddling and should be especially aware of possi-

123

A calculated risk—let good judgment be your guide whenever afloat.

ble changes in river levels and how such changes can affect the difficulty of the run. In many parts of the country, the water levels in popular rivers are monitored by the Forest Service, Department of Water Resources, or a similar agency to determine the flow rate, or level, often expressed in cubic feet per second (cfs). Supplementing these sources, boaters knowledgeable about a particular river can advise you what the cfs level means: for example, at 3,000 cfs this river is considered "squirrely" and demanding in the extreme, at 1,800 it is ideal, at 900 it becomes highly technical (meaning, lots of rocks to dodge), and below 600 there is not enough water to run it. Of course, knowing the cfs level without knowing the size of the watercourse or its gradient is about as useful as knowing the barometer reading without knowing whether it is rising or falling or which way the wind is blowing.

## KNOW THE HAZARDS

Four basic canoeing hazards have killer potential: cold water, high water, sweepers, and reversals, the last three associated with moving water.

### Cold Water

Depending on the season, cold water can be a problem anywhere, be it a local frog pond, a large lake, or a river. In some parts of the country, because of latitude or snowmelt (my own northwest rivers, for example), cold water is a hazard year round.

In cold water the normal human body loses heat thirty-two times faster than in air of comparable temperature, and life expectancy in 33- to 40-degree water can be as little as fifteen minutes. The danger is a condition called "hypothermia," which is the specific result of exposure to cold. Hypothermia usually follows the initial panic or shock of immersion, which literally takes away the breath, strains the heart, and quickly numbs the extremities. Signs of hypothermia are a subnormal temperature within the body core and the inability of the body to produce heat. The skin and nearby tissues cool fast, and the shutting down of peripheral circulation to the extremities causes heaviness and numbness. Survival depends on many variables, including water temperature and the victim's size, fat content, and activity. In advanced stages of hypothermia, unconsciousness develops as the core body temperature drops to 90 degrees Fahrenheit. When the temperature drops to 85 degrees, the heart fails.

High water is a potential hazard because it increases the river's power and, in addition, means cold water during spring runoff. Since the difficulty of rescue increases proportionately with the flow rate, boaters should always be aware of the possibility of a sudden rise in water levels, as a result of sun on snow pack, heavy rains, or a dam release.

## Sweepers

Among experienced boaters, the hazard most feared and most capable of bringing all senses to full alert is the sweeper or strainer. This may be brush, a fallen tree, bridge pilings, or anything else that allows the water current to pass through but would pin the boater or boat to the obstacle. The water pressure in even a moderate current can be overwhelming to the entrapped person or boat, making rescue difficult if not impossible. The hazard is all the more insidious because of the lack of fanfare announcing its presence—unlike white water, which transmits obvious signals of potential danger. Scouting, local

Sweepers and strainers.

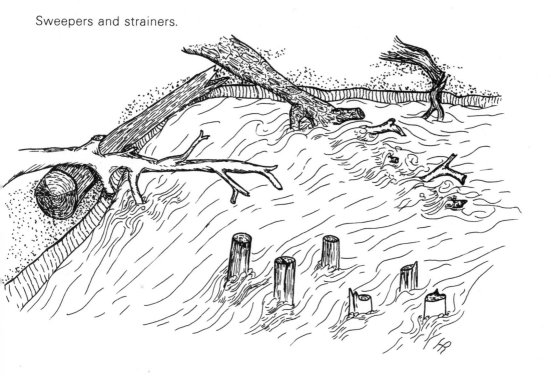

Holes.

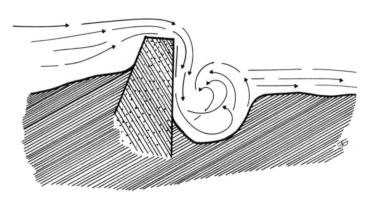

Reversal.

knowledge, alertness, and total avoidance are the best defense. There are few rapids whose dangers can rival that of a seemingly innocuous tree recently toppled into a river by a spring storm.

Early-season runs present the greatest danger, owing to the high likelihood of storm-related debris and the lack of traffic. No boaters will be able to give you a scouting report. Of course, a storm at any time of year or sudden surges in water levels can put trees and roots into the river. Certain rivers may be prone to debris at any time, owing to heavy forest cover, unstable or loose soil, or consistent high volume of water flows. And certain river sections such as headwaters, braided channels in the lower sections (alluvial deposits and unstable soils), and the outsides of bends will also be more likely to contain sweepers. If a clear and obvious passage cannot be seen, at the first sign of a sweeper, boaters should pull into shore, scout the obstruction, and determine whether portaging, lining, or a cautious paddling route is called for.

For the very experienced boater, white-water obstacles, including reversals and holes, can provide good sport. But they can quickly become hazardous. The most dangerous reversals occur below weirs, or low dams—often deceptive because of the seemingly unimpressive drop—causing the surface water actually to be going upstream. This action can indefinitely trap a canoe or person between the drop and the reversal wave. In the most serious reversals or holes ("souse holes" in the extreme form), a swimmer's only hope may be to dive below the surface to find the current flowing downstream.

## KNOW YOURSELVES

A realistic appraisal of your own physical and canoeing capabilities, in relation to the waters to be canoed, should keep you out of trouble. Being a good swimmer is no assurance of immunity and may well create a false sense of security. On the other hand, there is no reason why nonswimmers cannot actively pursue canoeing, unless they are nonswimmers because they fear the water. Being comfortable around water, knowing how to float or tread water, having faith in the buoyancy of both a swamped canoe and a life preserver, and being knowledgeable in other safety fundamentals can be adequate for the marginal swimmer.

One of the first rules of safe canoeing is never to canoe alone. On wilderness trips or on white water of Class II or above, three boats are a sensible minimum. Those who do canoe alone must be fully aware of the consequences and know themselves and their capabilities exceedingly well. In my experience, there are few who make the grade.

Knowing the boating capabilities of your companions is extremely important too. More than a few canoers have had to risk their own lives in an attempt to save another boater. The participation of marginal boaters in a given trip, be it one day or a month, depends on the composite skills of the group. In other words, one marginal boater in a party of ten strong ones would be acceptable, while two out of four is risky.

## KNOW YOUR EQUIPMENT

Start with a safe boat, one that is equal to the water to be navigated and matched to your own skills. It should be sound of hull, buoyant, and free from sharp corners and projections such as nails, rivets, or bolts. Open white-water

A throw rope should be carried on river trips.

canoes should have extra flotation and although it is important to have bow and stern lines, these and other lines—in fact, anything that might cause entanglement when you come out of the boat, like a spray skirt that won't release or buckles or clothing that might catch or snag—need to be well stowed or secured. Also, canoe seats that are too low and hang onto the heels are uncomfortable and potentially dangerous.

C-1's should be fitted with a simple-to-release spray skirt, grab loops at least six inches in diameter on both bow and stern, and a stern painter seven to eight feet long, secured by a quick-releasing S hook of coat-hanger wire just behind the cockpit. Grab loops and painter provide the means for self-rescue as well as for the rescue of other boaters.

Another important safety accessory for white-water boaters is a throw rope, 15 to 25 feet long. Have it ready when suspected water is approached. In addition to being a potential lifeline to a swimmer, it can also be used to winch a boat off a boulder.

PFDs, or life preservers, were covered in chapter 2, but their importance to safe boating cannot be overemphasized. For club trips, the leader should carry basic first-aid supplies, and for longer trips a comprehensive kit, perhaps assembled with the help of a family doctor. Choose clothing either for protection from cold or against the sun and its reflected rays. Wool is the best protection against cold water—even when wet—but a wet suit is a necessity for white-water boaters when water temperatures are in the sixties or below. Whether to choose a full-length or shorty wet suit, and of ⅛ or ⅜ inch thickness, will depend on the water and air temperatures expected—the heavier full suit gives more protection. Avoid nylon and cotton, which, when wet, act as a wick to carry heat away from the body.

Light shoes of some sort should be worn as protection both in and out of the boat, and in case of a white-water swim. For head protection, closed boaters require helmets; increasingly, open canoe white-water boaters are wearing them too.

## TAKING CARE OF YOURSELF

Recreational canoeing on protected waters is not a strenuous sport. The physical motions of canoeing are natural, and every stroke is followed by a free glide. And even though canoe tripping requires you to be reasonably fit, it is possible to plan a trip's itinerary to work your way to fitness as the trip progresses. Most people return from a one- or two-week trip feeling harder and fitter than ever before in their lives.

For those of you who plan to do a lot of white-water boating or expedition canoeing, good physical conditioning is a must, not only to meet the emergencies but in order to increase your enjoyment of the sport. Serious racers, whether flat-water, downriver, or slalom, are in top physical condition. On an NBC Special, "The Fittest of Them All," three top U.S. kayakers competed against seven other "mountainmen"—runners and climbers—in an eight-event competition. The first- and second-place winners, Chuck Lyda and Tom Ruwitch, were kayakers, with Eric Evans, a former U.S. Team coach and perennial top finisher in international kayak competition, coming in sixth. The result was no surprise to kayakers and canoers familiar with the rigors of slalom racing.

(Evans, who has written several books on kayaking and is a regular contributor to outdoors magazines, is something of an evangelist on the subject of training, recommending a regimen of on-the-water and dry-land workouts, including weight training and aerobic exercises such as biking, running, and cross-country skiing. Most canoers are not going to need that degree of preparedness, but, as with paddling skills, your physical conditioning should be matched against the activity contemplated.)

## Self-Preservation

Self-preservation and self-rescue need to be considered regardless of the level of canoeing challenge sought. Being around water is reason enough. To start with, prevention is always better than cure, so you can increase your odds by being a competent swimmer with the ability to handle yourself underwater. Always wear a PFD, keep your canoe in control, and be able to stop or reach shore before danger is encountered. Don't enter a rapid unless you are reasonably sure you can navigate it, and, in any event, be prepared to swim the entire rapid if you should go over.

A proper canoe has adequate buoyancy to support several people when fully swamped, so you should stay with your boat as long as it is practical. In a lake, if the distance from capsize to shore is beyond your swimming capability, stay with the boat. In a river you should also stay with the boat, unless you are putting yourself in even greater danger because of cold water or the approach of a violent rapid. Then get to shore or into an eddy as soon as possible. Whatever you do, hang onto your paddle! It will be hard to find, otherwise, and you will need it to get out.

Implicit in the success of any self-rescue strategy is not to panic. If you

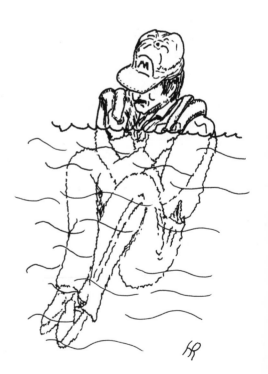

HELP position.

are in open water with the water temperature suggesting the danger of hypo-thermia and the decision has already been made that shore is out of swimming reach, observe these procedures. Do not thrash around. The body loses the greatest amount of heat in the groin, armpits and sides, back of the neck, and head, and your clothing holds a certain amount of warm air (wool especially), providing flotation and protection. Exercise such as treading water causes the body to lose heat faster, so the trick is to keep still. Assuming you have a good buoyant PFD, you can climb back into the capsized boat or assume the fetal-like Heat Escape Lessening Posture (HELP), keeping as much of the head and neck above water as possible. Do not swim unless there is absolutely no chance of rescue and you are certain you can make it.

If you capsize in the rapids, stay *upstream* of the canoe and leave it only if it will improve your safety. Avoid the danger of being pinned between a swamped canoe and an obstacle such as a boulder. If forced to swim the rapids, go on your back, feet first, keeping your toes up. Never try standing up in fast water unless it is too shallow for swimming. Think of the same ferrying tech-niques used in paddling and watch for helpful eddies or slack water as you try to work your way toward shore. If you are not alone, one of your boating companions should try to get to you at the bottom of the drop, so that you can grab a painter or grab loop as he attempts to ferry you toward shore. This requires tremendous effort on the part of the rescuer—you will be dragging like a sea anchor—so try to help by kicking and swimming.

## TAKING CARE OF OTHERS

The trickiest proposition in boating safety is knowing when to attempt a rescue, as well as what to do. Overly ambitious, or hasty, poorly conceived rescue attempts have often resulted in the rescuer's getting into trouble too. Attempts should be made from the safety of a boat by the strongest boater, or boaters, or preferably from shore, using an extended paddle or throwing line. Canoe clubs, camps, and training clinics teach canoe rescue techniques and how to deal with a swamped canoe, righting and emptying a canoe in both deep and shallow water, and techniques for extricating canoes trapped in fast water. It is worthwhile training, but only good judgment and experience should be your guide as to what constitutes a vain or self-endangering rescue attempt, be it of a boat or a boater.

A reality of white-water boating is that when a boater goes over in the rapids, there is no real possibility of rescue until boater and boat wash out at the bottom, and by then all that can go wrong will have gone wrong. So at the first opportunity for rescue, you must be ready to móve quickly, using a throw line, or having a bow or stern line that the swimmer can grab. If a throw line is used from shore, it may be belayed around a tree or boulder.

You do not have to spend a lot of time in formal practice of rescue techniques unless you expect to spend a lot of time on white water, yet there are many opportunities to "play" with a capsized canoe to gain confidence in its buoyancy. Families, in particular, should spend some time in shallow, warm water, tipping the canoe over purposely, clambering in and out, making a game of seeing how many people it can support, and, finally, practicing emptying the canoe in deep and shallow water. The lesson is that aside from the techniques themselves a capsized canoe is no big deal. It happens. People do get wet. Just hang on to your canoe as if it were a big air mattress.

Throw line and tree belay.

Playing with a swamped canoe gives these kids confidence in their craft.

# FIRST AID

We cannot give a full course in first aid here, but some basic know-how in certain water-related or outdoors situations should be covered. You might consider the following questions:

1. *What is the treatment for hypothermia?*

Since hypothermia is caused by exposure to cold, treatment is aimed at warming the victim from the inside out. Move the victim to shelter and warmth as rapidly as possible. Remove all wet clothes and apply heat to the central body core (no one ever died of cold hands or feet!) with hot water bottles or an electric blanket. In a remote situation, just putting a victim in a sleeping bag or wrapping in a blanket may not be sufficient, since, by definition, hypothermia victims are unable to generate their own heat. Thus an external source is necessary. An effective field measure is for one or two of the rescuers to remove their own clothing and use their own bodies to warm the victim's naked body. A sleeping bag or blanket should be used to conserve the body heat.

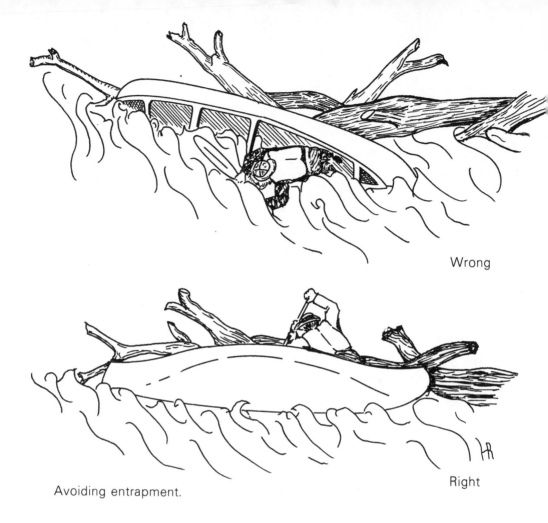

Wrong

Avoiding entrapment.

Right

If the victim appears dead, CPR*, including heart massage and mouth-to-mouth resuscitation, should be administered. All hypothermia victims should be seen by a doctor as soon as possible, since there are possible serious aftereffects associated with shock and the buildup of lactic acid in the system.

Unless conscious and able to take hot liquids, a victim should not be given anything to drink, especially not alcohol. The cold extremities should not be rubbed, as this merely diverts blood and heat away from the core. Do not wrap a hypothermic in a blanket without an auxiliary source of heat, unless it is for protection against further heat loss before treatment.

---

*Cardio-pulmonary resuscitation; the trip leader or some member of the canoeing party should have this training, especially on remote or difficult trips.

2. *Your canoe is suddenly being swept broadside into a log (sweeper). What*
   *should you do?*

Lean downstream—toward the log—and attempt to hurl yourself over the log. You want to avoid exposing your open hull to the current, and avoid having both you and your boat sucked under the log or tree, where limbs and branches might entrap you with their "strainer" effect.

3. *A canoeing accident has occurred on a local river. One of the victims appears*
   *to be without pulse or respiration when pulled from the water. What is the best*
   *method of artificial respiration, and how is it applied?*

The quickest and easiest method is mouth-to-mouth breathing and closed chest massage—CPR.

4. *While cooking dinner over a campfire, you accidentally pick up a hot spoon,*
   *burning your fingers. They are red and very sore. What now?*

Plunge them into cold water and hold them there until the burning stops and the pain lessens.

5. *You have finished your day's paddle and the takeout is a steep incline. You*
   *dislodge a rock which bounces down and hits your partner on the head. He*
   *falls and rolls a short distance. What should you do?*

Try not to move him until you determine the extent of his injuries. If he is conscious, inquire how he feels. Check for bleeding, breathing, and give first aid as required. If there is pallor and general weakness accompanied by a rapid pulse, the victim may be in shock. Nausea or vomiting may indicate a more severe case, and a cold and clammy body which goes into violent shaking with chattering teeth may indicate severe shock. In shock, heart and brain are suffering from a deficiency of blood, so place the victim in a near-horizontal position, feet slightly higher than head. In shock there is rapid loss of body heat, so the victim should be covered, top and bottom, with blankets or available garments. A little fluid (but no alcohol) may help if the victim is conscious. Beyond this, a doctor's treatment is called for. Transport to the hospital as soon as possible.

6. *Your child is fishing and suddenly cries out that he has a fish hook in his*
   *finger. What should you do?*

Push the hook through the skin completely; cut off the barb and pull out the hook. Flush the wound well with an antiseptic solution. Make sure tetanus shot is up to date.

# Canoe Tripping

To many, canoe tripping is the sole reason for canoeing. A canoe trip provides challenge, relaxation, discovery, and the pleasure of a real-life adventure. There are still many unspoiled waterways; perhaps more rivers and wild areas will be set aside to be enjoyed by the self-propelled traveler. Many possibilities for canoe tripping also exist along populated waterways. A canoe trip may combine historical interest, physical challenge, and scenic beauty. Fishing, searching for wildlife, picture-taking, or just plain loafing are added attractions.

## THE CREW

Canoe tripping may give you the camaraderie of summer camp, a satisfying wilderness experience with other men and women, or a more interdependent life-style for your family. Give a lot of thought to the makeup of your group. When you think about spending three days, a week, or a month seldom more than 17 feet away from your companions, you can see why your choice of crew is important.

To many, tripping is the real joy of canoeing.

The chemistry of your canoe-tripping crew is very important.

Slovenliness is certainly not what you're looking for in a canoeing companion, but too-great concern about being clean and freshly groomed can make for even more annoyance. If your prospective partner has a fussy palate, or a low tolerance for physical discomfort, think twice about spending your hard-earned vacation in his or her company. You may be even worse off with a macho type whose risk-taking can get you both into trouble. Happiness in canoe tripping is a judicious blend of adventuresomeness and good sense.

## PLANNING THE TRIP

Assuming you have the necessary paddling skills for a trip and are fortunate enough to have convinced your family or some compatible comrades to join you, it's time to make plans. And planning, like getting there, can be half the fun.

Little steps and then big steps is the way to approach canoe tripping, especially if you are going to involve the family. The three-day trip with two overnights is a good warmer-upper; it's the time to find out if you know how to carry a canoe, if the tents and rain gear are watertight, if Susie is allergic to down or your hand-picked bow partner is scared of the dark. You need all the same gear—just less food—for a three-day trip as you do for two weeks, so it's perfect practice. And the penalty for leaving something behind will be only a temporary inconvenience.

## Where to Go

Affiliation with a canoe club provides access to a source of ideas, as well as to scheduled trips organized by club members, but if you're a do-it-yourselfer, you have a project ahead. Your crew's proficiency and time are going to be your limiting factors. You will probably be looking for something within a reasonable traveling distance from home. The amount of time you plan to spend on your canoe trip should have some bearing on how much time is devoted to getting there. Driving fourteen hours to take a three-day trip is a waste of energy. Expedition planning is discussed in the next chapter; for now, let's look at the kinds of canoe trips for which there is readily available information, such as guidebooks or canoe maps, and organized facilities such as canoe rentals, designated campsites, or wilderness preserves, all or partially protected for canoeists. Moving clockwise around North America, such areas would include Algonquin Park in Ontario, the Boundary Waters Canoe Area (Quetico Park–Superior National Forest) shared by Ontario and Minnesota, the Allagash Wilderness Waterway in Maine, the Adirondack Preserve in New York, the Okefenokee Swamp in Florida and Georgia, the Buffalo National River in Arkansas, the National Scenic Riverways in the Ozarks, the Guadalupe in Texas, the John Day in Oregon, or the Upper Missouri in the Charles M. Russell National Wildlife Range in Montana, to name just a few.

For your first canoe trip, there is a lot to be said for heading to one of the more popular areas specifically designated for canoeing. There is comfort in having others around, and if you're taking little kids along, civilization nearby is reassuring.

### Information Sources

A comprehensive listing of information sources for canoeing would fill an entire book. Fortunately, such a book exists. In an obvious labor of love, a librarian at Washington State University has compiled the most comprehensive up-to-date compendium on the subject ever published, *Wilderness Waterway: A Guide to Information Sources*. I am sorry that over the years I have not had the benefit of such a volume—but perhaps I would have missed out on some of the fun

There is a wealth of published information sources for the canoe tripper.

involved in the time-consuming, often frustrating, occasionally revelatory quest for useful, pertinent information.

Usually canoe dealers or liveries will have a rack of materials, including waterway guides for the region they serve. Canoe clubs are another excellent source; in addition to their schedules of organized trips, many of these clubs publish regular newsletters containing trip reports.

Every state and province of Canada has the equivalent of a Department of Tourism, and a letter or phone call will bring forth a blizzard of freebies, from which may be culled some useful information. A better source seems to be state Departments of Fish and Game, Natural Resources, Lands and Forests, or Parks and Recreation.

## Maps
Two excellent sources for maps are the United States Geological Survey, 2201 Sunrise Valley Drive, Reston, Virginia 22092, and the Department of Energy, Mines, and Resources, 615 Booth Street, Ottawa, Ontario K1A OE9, Canada. Both offer contour maps in a variety of scales but before ordering, you will need to obtain the indexes, specifying the scale (1:25,000, 1:50,000, 1:250,000, etc.), and/or state or province. These are provided at no charge and come with the map order forms.

Although the maps are quite detailed with respect to land contours and such geological features as swamps and glaciers, they often do not show recent road incursions or other development. So note the date of survey or revision. Also, they are not often accurate where rivers are concerned, depicting rapids that turn out to be nonexistent or totally ignoring a six-foot waterfall. However, a prospective route, once identified, can be researched through some of the other sources mentioned.

A more rational approach is to first identify a prospect from a guidebook or club source and then order the U.S.G.S. maps. For most of the waterways in the United States you will find the one-mile-to-the-inch (1:62,500) quadrangles to be most useful, whereas the more extensive regions of Canada are adequately displayed in the four-mile-to-the-inch (1:250,000) scale. A good number of the organized areas, such as the Boundary Waters Canoe Area or Algonquin Park, have special maps for the canoer, showing routes, portages, and even campsites.

## Magazines

Magazines such as *Canoe,* of course, cater specifically to the paddler; almost every issue contains an article about canoe tripping, somewhere in the world, and often a piece on waterways of a particular region or state. My favorite periodicals, in addition to *Canoe,* include *Backpacker/Adventure Travel, National Geographic,* and *Canadian Geographical Journal.*

And sometimes an inspiration is what you need. Years back, my wife and I happened to read Pierre Berton's spellbinding account of the greatest gold rush in history, *Klondike;* a year later our family launched two canoes on a tributary of the Yukon for a 500-mile journey to Dawson City.

In addition to the U.S.G.S. series, there are maps prepared especially for the canoeist.

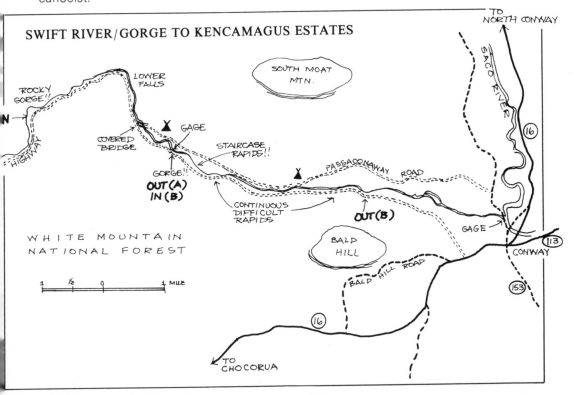

## When to Go

The traffic in popular canoeing areas can definitely detract from the solitude you seek, but peace and quiet can usually be found with a little ingenuity. Many times, research will reveal out-of-the-way access or egress points, and it may be well worth paying someone to shuttle you—perhaps by a motorboat tow—to get you and your crew off the overly beaten track. Even on popular routes it is possible to make short detours, up a side channel or around a corner into a secluded bay, where suddenly you are alone in your own little world.

Picking the time of year is very important too. Long-range weather predictions are hazardous, but one should have a reasonable idea of the weather patterns for the locale during the contemplated period of the trip. Having said that, consider trips before Memorial Day and after Labor Day; in both cases you are in and out before or after the bugs and people, and fishing is usually better early and late. July and August are the usual vacation months, so expect to find plenty of company, especially in organized canoeing areas. June before school lets out is a possibility, but in some parts of the Northeast it is the height of the blackfly season. Canoeing is full of compromises. I have taken canoe trips as early as April and as late as November. Any time can be great.

## How to Go

Every year the roads reach farther into the backcountry. This has unfortunate implications, but it also means that there are very few canoe trips (as opposed to expeditions) that are not accessible by automobile. In the organized areas, some outfitters and other local entrepreneurs will provide a shuttle, using either your vehicle, or theirs, or both. In areas without such services, make inquiries at the gas station, general store, or local branch of government. Of course, if your complement of crew and canoes is going to require more than one car, you may have to organize your own shuttle.

How many people and canoes? Three canoes is a good number, each carrying two adults, which gives you a minimum safety margin in case one canoe should be lost or destroyed, but I wouldn't discourage parties of four, two, or even a solo from making plans. Just take the risks into consideration, and prepare and plan accordingly. If your party includes small kids or women, a good 17-foot tripping canoe can safely accomodate three persons. You may be a bit cramped, but sometimes it is the only solution.

As the crew grows in size, there is one unalterable truth: The larger the party, the slower it moves. Unless the group is experienced and extremely well organized, the likelihood of things going awry increases geometrically. A certain amount of tranquillity is sacrificed when a small navy embarks on a canoe trip, and I usually associate devastated campsites with their passing. On the other hand, a large group can be lots of fun. Some years ago, our family joined four other families and a dozen canoes for five days in the Adirondacks, managing to pack in a whole range of social and outdoor activities. We used the base-camp approach—in this case a large and comfortable campsite—so that those who wished to stay close to the hearth could do so. Others departed on fishing excursions, hikes, wildflower gathering, or mud-pie making.

### The Trip Leader

What about a leader? From my experience, if a strong leader is called for, you probably have the wrong crew, and if you have to bludgeon any prospective member into helping plan the trip, you've got a problem before the paddles are wet. James Fenimore Cooper's Pathfinder was always referring to various persons' "gifts," and with good luck you may find a crew of leaders with a "gift" for each of the divisions of labor comprising the canoe-tripping experience: paddling, portering, tent raising, wood gathering, fireplace building, fishing, cooking, dishwashing, storytelling, and weather forecasting.

# FOOD AND GEAR

If you enjoyed researching the "where" and "when," you're going to love planning the "what." As months turn to days and departure time nears, I make and remake my lists, organize and reorganize the menu. Despite having done this for twenty years, the fun endures. No matter how often you have been through it, you must have a complete list and then make sure every item is checked off as you pack it into the car. Many a canoe trip has found itself well downriver sans what one friend calls *le papier nécessaire*.

Durability and water repellence are the bywords for canoe-tripping gear. Weight is important but, except on the portage trail, it is far less critical than for the backpacker or biker. Canoeing equipment is subjected to rougher treatment: loaded and unloaded, stuffed and unstuffed, sat upon and mauled at canoe and campsite. The ultra-light gear of the backpacker has a short life expectancy on a canoe trip.

## Canoes and Paddles

A good tripping canoe should be able to take abuse, weigh no more than 80 pounds, and be capable of carrying at least two full-sized paddlers and 300 pounds or more of food and gear. A center thwart rigged for a one-person carry with a paddle yoke or built-in yoke is a must. A good length of sturdy line in both bow and stern for lining, tracking, and securing is needed, as well as the usual sponge or bailer. A couple of sticks and perhaps the spare paddle on the bottom of the canoe will keep duffel off the floor, where the inevitable puddles eventually find their way through all but the most watertight packs.

Your paddles, which will end up being used as poles, levers, shovels, scythes, and filet boards, should be tough but light, so they don't feel like crowbars by day's end. A broken paddle can be a hassle, so in addition to choosing for durability, an extra for each canoe is good insurance. If you go with a synthetic paddle, some flex in the shaft is desirable. Avoid those with rubber coverings on the shaft—they are rough on the hands after several hours of paddling.

## Packs and Packing

The theory in canoe packing is to consolidate as much as possible into a few very heavy packs, durable enough to survive the constant abrasions and concussions from getting them into and out of the canoe and which permit you to move all the gear across a portage, or from canoe to campsite, with the fewest number of trips.

Duluth packs (far left) or similar large, soft packs are preferred to frame packs by most canoe trippers.

Although one manufacturer has come up with a large-volume frame pack specifically designed for canoe tripping, most backpacks are too flimsy, too limited in capacity, and too restricted by a frame that is always in the way when you are trying to load the canoe. The ideal and traditional pack for tripping is still the Duluth pack, a giant envelope of heavy canvas, blessed with wide leather straps and, on the better models, a tumpline which allows you to support some of the weight with your head. In this way you can carry bulky, overweight loads for distances up to a mile, and, lined with heavy-duty garbage bags, doubled up, or with rubberized waterproof bags, your food and gear are well protected. One Duluth pack can carry two sleeping bags, sleeping mats, a tent, and an ax, and still have room to stuff the rain gear under the flap. Another pack can carry almost a week's food for a party of four. Depending on whether you are carrying gear or food, a Duluth may weigh from 45 to 125 pounds.

In addition to your workhorses, you will need some specialized packs, including one or more of the waterproof boxes or bags discussed in chapter 2. If there are kids in the crew, consider smaller packs that will not overload or endanger them. In fact, one manufacturer makes a nylon Duluth pack (a Klamath pack) with a plastic liner that weighs less than half the canvas ones. Duffel bags make good canoe packs and can either be fitted with a tumpline or stacked on top of another pack for a short stagger across a portage.

Very useful is a rigid, boxlike container, or "wanigan," which can carry daily implements such as pots and pans, utensils, a small tool kit, toilet paper, stove, matches, candles, file, and a few food items such as salt and pepper, plus the bread and makings for the next lunch stop. In short, it is a common repository for all the frequently needed cooking and camp items, so that once under way you will be able to avoid the dig-and-search routine.

To keep your gear dry, use a waterproof liner and see that the packs are slightly raised off the floor of the canoe. To preserve your low center of gravity, the weight needs to be concentrated toward the center of the canoe, with as little showing above the gunwale line as possible. Prudence also calls for tying or strapping in your gear, particularly if you're planning to run some rapids.

## Clothing and Personal Gear

Most of what you need is probably already in your closet, and, exclusive of footwear, what you take should fit into a sleeping-bag-sized stuff bag. Plenty of socks are a must, ideally of wool or a wool blend. You'll need a regular change of socks and underwear, a couple of pairs of pants, an old work shirt, and perhaps a pair of shorts or swim trunks. If cool weather will be encountered, include a PolarGuard vest or a sweater. Wool shirts or sweaters are preferred to cotton since wool is warm even when wet. The same holds true for PolarGuard and Fiberfill II, making it preferable to down around water. Pants can be of denim or khaki, never corduroy, and lightweight for fast drying. In cold or wet climates, wool would be better.

Follow the layered approach to dressing; rather than wearing one heavy garment, don and doff several light shirts or sweaters, as temperatures and your level of activity require. Remember too that your PFD, topped by a windbreaker or rain shirt, acts as an effective insulator and substitute for a warm vest. The only other special items to consider are a hat, brimmed for wet weather or wool for cold; a couple of bandannas, for wiping everything from runny noses to knife blades; and a pair of work gloves. Old-timers swear by a change of socks. When you're cold, wet, or just plain fatigued, it's a great boost to the morale, and it really works.

## Rain Gear

Without a doubt, rain gear is the single most important piece of clothing on a canoe trip. You can make do in lots of other areas, but why court misery? The old standby is the army poncho, which can also double as a tarp or ground cloth. It should have strong grommets at the corners and unfailing side snaps. Billowing over a fire, a poncho is a hazard around the campsite, so it should be belted or tied at the waist. It's nice to wrap your knees up in one as you paddle, but in the canoe it can become a sail-in-reverse when the wind blows. A poncho is also a bit ungainly if you are packing over a portage.

A full rain suit with hood is a better choice, but avoid the extreme lightweight suits which lack the durability for the rough regimen of a canoe trip and often end up leaking. A rain shirt with a minimum of zippers and snaps is a good choice, or you may wish to pay top dollar for a quality rain jacket. Some of the new Gore-Tex designs are excellent, and if you do a conscientious job of applying the seam sealer, they give unfailing rain protection with a minimum of condensation. Chaps are a lightweight and economical alternative to rain pants, but they are a compromise.

## Footwear

Many a canoe trip will incorporate some hiking, but hiking boots, as such, suffer a number of drawbacks as canoeing gear. Unless they are of the very lightweight klettershoe or "waffle stomper" variety, they are almost impossible to dry out in a reasonable amount of time. Resign yourself to the fact that your footwear is going to spend some time in the water. In ascending order of preference, one should consider inexpensive work boots, well oiled or treated for water repellence; waterproof boots such as the Dunhams (very expensive); or rubber-bottomed 6- to 8-inch boots with leather uppers, such as Bean's Maine Hunting Shoe. The last are reasonably inexpensive, compared to a hiking boot, and come with a removable felt innersole that can be put into the bottom of your sleeping bag to dry at night.

Your boots will be fine around a rough campsite or on the portage trail, but for a change of shoes, an old pair of fast-drying tennis shoes is the answer. If the day's mileage calls for little rivers or scratchy rapids and the inevitable wading, these are the shoes. And, waiting dry in your pack, if you are fortunate, they are a pleasant change for evening around the camp.

## Shelter

"Why live like a mole?" That was the rhetorical question years ago of a custom tentmaker who produced a unique tepeelike design in a little establishment under the el in upper Manhattan. He had a good point, and it is even truer today with the advent of versatile, lightweight fabrics for tents and rain flies.

Without the same weight constraints as the hiker, it makes sense to opt for the most spacious and rain-repellent shelter available. On a full-fledged expedition to the Northwest Territories, plagued by hordes of blackflies and mosquitoes which were tenacious beyond belief, we carried large six-person domes. In the evening our entire crew could escape inside with dinner, while the little devils pelted like raindrops against the nylon tent fabric.

There are more tent designs than we can adequately cover in this volume, but some general thoughts may be useful. Simple designs are best: A-frames, semi-wall, miner's tent, Baker, or the new Quonset and dome shapes, which set

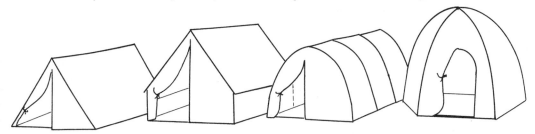

A-frame, semi-wall, Quonset and dome designs make good canoe shelter.

up quickly with fiberglass wands and a minimum of guy lines. Look for models with small-gauge mosquito netting and lighter colors that tend to be more cheerful. The new lightweight tents usually come with an easy-to-erect rain fly and provide for adequate ventilation even if they are drenched by rain. Or you may do as we did, extending the life of our ten-year-old nylon A-frame by sewing a rain fly for it, using coated rip-stop nylon and a commercially available grommet kit.

Unless you are going to be sitting in a base camp, ease of setup and takedown is an important feature. Late in the day, as dusk gives way to darkness and rain clouds threaten, too much time spent with Tinker-Toy frames and tangled tent lines can be disheartening. Before you take off, set the tent up in the backyard, count all the tent stakes, guy lines, and poles, and check for torn grommets and decayed netting. Consider subjecting it to a summer thunderstorm to make sure it is going to keep you dry. If it's a new tent, this is the time to learn the idiosyncrasies of setup and takedown, rather than under the anxious eyes of a paddle-weary crew.

## Sleeping Bags and Mats

Your choice of a fully cut, square-bottomed bag or a tubular mummy type is a matter of sleeping habits and preference, but the same comments made about tents concerning spaciousness versus weight considerations are applicable to bags. Choose either a high- or low-temperature rating, depending on where and during what season you plan to take your canoe trip. The size of your pocket-book may dictate the quality of construction, baffle-sewn being superior to sewn-through, and down-filled better than synthetic. A fine-quality down sleeping bag is a joy and delight forever, featuring maximum loft (which means more dead air space and consequent warmth) at the least weight and bulk. But down is expensive, somewhat fragile, and, if soaked, almost useless. I would tend to stay away from the cheap fillers. Consider, instead, the fine bags being made with PolarGuard and Fiberfill II—trade names of the fiber manufacturers—for they are considerably less expensive than their down counterparts. They compress and stuff with a little more effort than down, and while there is a modest weight penalty (for equivalent warmth), they provide warmth even when wet and can withstand a lot of abuse.

Inflatable air mattresses mean comfort, and they can tame the most rugged terrain. However, an air mat of sufficiently heavy construction to resist punctures or midnight expiration carries a big weight penalty. Also, getting all the air out as you hurry to break camp in the morning can be a hassle, and in cold weather they conduct the cold.

Foam pads are a suitable alternative. They are warmer, and there is no need to worry about punctures. The most comfortable ones are about two inches thick, with an open-cell foam bonded to a thinner closed-cell layer, all encased in a nylon cover. Another ingenious new product is a self-inflating mat which combines the warmth of foam with the comfort of air and is proclaimed by some of my canoeing friends to be a true advancement in the state of the art of outdoor sleeping.

## Camp and Kitchen Gear

Some of the organized canoeing areas are likely to restrict the cutting of firewood and firebuilding, and that's a shame, for the campfire is a traditional and integral part of canoe tripping. Unfortunately, that's the price we pay for years of abusing our wild areas.

In restricted areas, or where wood is just plain scarce, you will need to carry a stove. Fortunately, the popularity of backpacking has led to the development and refinement of a plethora of models which use a variety of fuels such as propane, kerosene, alcohol, and regular gas. Because of less worry about weight, canoers tend to eat heartier than backpackers, so it is appropriate to shop for the more powerful, heavy-duty models. Two popular ones are the Optimus IIIB, a kerosene burner, and the Phoebus 625, which uses white gas. You will need priming pastes for these, and your fuel should be carried in an absolutely leak-proof container designed for the purpose. As with the tents, a few practice sessions at home before you depart for the outback may spare you some anxious moments on the trail.

If you are fortunate enough to travel in an area where campfires are permitted, leave the stove at home. Even on heavily trafficked canoe routes, there is much drift- and downed wood to be found. This is especially true along the rivers. A small fire requiring less wood is environmentally smart, and much more efficient for cooking. Some organized areas already have fireplaces and grates in place; less developed routes will retain the handiwork of other travelers. It is wise to carry your own grill or fire irons, sturdy enough to support a four- to six-quart pot.

If there is an insufficient or improperly oriented windbreak, you may have to erect one. Some times a propped-up canoe is the ticket. In windy or rainy conditions you will need a windbreak for the stove as well, or the heat from your flame will be quickly dissipated—a great fuel waster.

For your fire, you will need tinder to light it, either manufactured (such as Hexamine tablets, candles, or waxed paper) or foraged, as well as tools for cutting and splitting firewood. A folding saw for cutting 18-inch logs and a small Hudson's Bay ax for splitting (hatchets are ineffective and dangerous) will do the trick nicely. Running the Middle Fork of the Salmon, we discovered that our saw and ax had been forgotten. There was a plentiful supply of driftwood, and we remedied our oversight by using soccer-ball-sized rocks to reduce the larger pieces to fireplace dimensions. This involved leaning the oversized limb against a rock and hurling our boulder down on it, making sure to get our toes out of the way.

Nesting pots and a juice container, accompanied by a spatula, serving spoon, and can opener, will comprise the cooking gear, and I suggest plastic bowls rather than the metal plates which usually come with cook kits. For grabbing hot pots, try a sturdy pair of goosenecked pliers instead of the unreliable handles that come with the nesting pots. They can serve a lot of other camp uses as well.

Depending on how strong a back you have or the number of portages you expect to encounter, there is a limitless amount of other paraphernalia you can tote along, from teddy bears to guitars. Radios and lanterns are incompatible with canoe tripping, but desirable options would include fishing equipment, a camera, and, for wind- or rain-bound camps, a deck of cards or paperback book. Binoculars seem to make sense but end up rarely being used. Flashlights, like lanterns, create a dependency, but are not of great value. They add weight and are superfluous during the summer when daylight comes at 4:30 A.M. and stays until 9 or 10 at night. A small spiral notepad and ballpoint pen are inexpensive, and if you are diligent in recording the day's events you will cherish the recall of otherwise forgotten details—the happenings and misadventures that are all part of the canoe-tripping experience.

## Food

Canoe trippers travel on their stomachs. The length of the canoe trip and the degree of difficulty (usually measured by the number of portages!) will determine the type of camp kitchen and food you will carry. On one month-long trip down a swift but unobstructed river, we went 500 miles without a portage. Although we carried a great many freeze-dried meals, we were able to add canned goods and condiments, as weight was not the primary consideration. It's nice to be able to produce something extravagant for dinner after weeks of eating dehydrated fare.

For a weekend or short trip, anything goes, from ice chests full of steaks to a spartan diet of dried fruit and nuts. Where to buy the food? The grocery store has it all: everything from canned bacon, instant milk, oatmeal, dried fruit, and soup to packaged dinners, "helpers," and such standbys as Kraft or Chef Boy-ar-dee spaghetti and meat sauce.

For a longer trip dictating foods of less weight and bulk, consider light-weight prepackaged foods, dehydrated or freeze dried. There are several names to choose from, including Rich Moor, Chuck Wagon, Stow-A-Way, Mountain House, and Wilson. By ordering in quantity and then repacking the food in single-meal units, you can lower per-serving costs. Mountain House, for example, packages a full line of excellent freeze-dried food in No. 10 cans. The price is still high but not as bad as the meal-sized pack. If you need just a few lightweight meals, your local sporting goods store can probably supply your needs.

Be organized when you pack your grub. The supermarket staples, including dried milk, oatmeal, Tang, rice, instant mashed potatoes, coffee, and sugar, should be removed from their boxes, bags, or bottles and repackaged in double or triple Baggies (or Ziploc bags), put into a cloth bag, and labeled with Magic Marker. Tubes or plastic bottles are available from most backpacking suppliers, and into these go peanut butter, honey, and catsup. If there is more than one boat in your group, be sure to divide the food evenly between the boats, with approximately equal days' meals in each.

You may find the consistency and flavor of trail foods somewhat bland and uniform, although they have improved tremendously in the past few years. Consequently, you might spice up your food pack with seasonings such as onion flakes, bell peppers, parsley, curry powder, bouillon cubes, salt and pepper—in fact, anything you like to use at home.

Store-bought bread tends to crush and crumble, if it survives the midnight raids of the squirrels and raccoons. One answer is bannock or trail bread. Ingredients are all measured and premixed at home and packed in plastic bags. Pull out a bag and add just enough water to make a kneadable blob. Mix this in the bag and spread the blob in a frying pan for over-the-fire cooking or in a loaf pan for reflector-oven baking. When using a frypan, just prop the pan in front of the fire, after the bottom is done, and bake until the top is golden brown.

## Canoe Trail Ecology

How do you clean up the mess? Pam sprayed on the inside of pots and pans before use helps them come clean. For general dishwashing, we heat water in the biggest pot, add some dish soap (biodegradables for campers are available), then rinse well and dry. For larger groups on an outing of a week or more, it would be a wise precaution to boil all the silverware, cups, and dishes (without soap) periodically.

S.O.S. can be used for heavy scouring, but don't be too concerned about getting all the black off the pots. Use the plastic bag that the last meal was packed in to cover the pot before it is nested up.

This leads us into the subject of canoe trail ecology. Too many people, too much garbage, too much soapsuds: It all adds up. Where there is an abundance of moving water, your cleaning activities are quickly flushed into oblivion if you are using biodegradable soaps. In heavily trafficked areas and on smaller waterways, one needs to be more attentive to the potential for polluting. That which can be burned should be burned. A small pit lined with stones can serve as your "drain field" for the dirty dishwater. In any case, that which cannot be burned, or flushed should be packed up and carried out. In many organized areas, plastic bags are provided (and even registered); the park overseers want to see them brought out full! We have traveled in some areas where these rules are stringently enforced—in one such area, fires must be built on a pan and the ashes carried out—and it's worth the effort. It seems a pity that bureaucratic rules have to be imposed on otherwise carefree outdoor pursuits, but the benefit is clean and appealing campsites where we can nurture the illusion, if not the reality, that we are their "discoverers."

Carrying out what you carry in doesn't apply only to your tin cans and soapsuds, either. A discarded tennis shoe, broken Styrofoam ice chest, or punctured air mat is just as unsightly as an empty Dinty Moore Beef Stew can. "Take only pictures, leave only footprints," is an overworn entreaty, but worth repeating.

What people take is almost as insidious as what they leave. Stripping the bark from trees, appropriating signs, privy doors, fire grates, and other public conveniences, is thoughtless and unnecessary. The Golden Rule is applicable here: Thoughtful canoe campers will leave a campsite in the same tidy condition that they would want to find after a good day's paddle, even if it means picking up after a sloppy predecessor.

## Drinking Water

Running water in sunlight purifies very quickly, and most larger bodies of water where one might plan a canoe trip are likely to be potable. If there is a question about the water, you may want to carry and use Halazone tablets (inexpensive and available at any drug store). Boiling water is even more effective. Water may be highly discolored or sedimented, but perfectly safe to drink. In these cases, if the taste or consistency repels you, your only solution may be to find a spring or feeder stream.

Assuming you have chosen an area and obtained good maps, it is time to plan the route. The critical factors, in addition to the proficiency of the crew, are total mileage, size and orientation of the lakes, number of portages (known and unknown), river gradients and obstacles such as falls, rapids, or dams that may have to be scouted, and, finally, the purpose of the trip itself. If relaxation and enjoyment of the fishing or scenery along the way is the goal, your mileage allowance will, of course, be conservative.

## The Strategy

A family group traveling through little lakes and streams, with a portage each day, may plan no more than 7 to 10 miles per day and allow for several layovers or rest days. A red-blooded group of men or women planning to descend a reasonably challenging river with known and unknown obstacles might consider 15 to 30 miles a day; any rest day would merely be a dividend paid for overachieving one day's anticipated mileage. Then, there are big rivers with gradient and few obstacles, where a five- to eight-mph current lets a canoeing party knock off 30 to 50 miles in a long day. After you have considered all the factors, add in some insurance, in any case.

In addition to your maps, you may consult with earlier parties, local sportsmen, or, in the case of organized areas, one of the outfitters. These sources should help you in marking out a route, including the nature and location of campsites, the likely and known obstacles or dangers on a particular river, the length, location, and condition of the portage trails, and the effect of present or recent water levels along your proposed route. Two months of rain, or an enterprising beaver, can significantly alter a water trail from that shown on the map. The most important thing to remember, however, is that after you have gathered all the best available advice, look upon it only as a clue. Even the most knowledgeable people, although desiring to be helpful, have memory blanks, or perceptions that would differ greatly from your own (or another expert's); in the final analysis, you must rely on yourself.

Prior to your mileage considerations, you may have to make some other strategy decisions, often dictated by the geography itself. A canoe trip can go point-to-point, such as a downriver trip; in a circle, which also maximizes the variety of scene while avoiding the need of a shuttle; or perhaps a partial circle, which may retrace part of the outbound route. One strategy, which may be particularly suited to a first-time or family crew, is the base-camp trip mentioned earlier. Here one seeks to find a large, comfortable site, offering as many indigenous attractions as possible, while permitting one-day or overnight excursions on foot or by canoe. The establishment of a well-organized and comfortable base permits more sedentary members of the group to read, swim, sunbathe, carve, or just putter while others take off on hiking, fishing, spelunking, photography, or white-water excursions. The peripatetic ones can return to a base which, with each passing day, becomes more comfortable.

## The Canoe Route

Traveling downriver, the problem obviously will not be one of "finding one's way" but, rather, knowing the location and severity of obstacles and when and where to get off the river to scout or to portage. You will also need to know the location of campsites and perhaps fresh water. If heavy rapids or a falls are to be encountered, you need to mark your map and know beforehand the landmarks that signal their imminence. These might include a noticeable elbow in the river's course, a tributary, an abandoned cabin, or a prominent outcropping of rock. Often a portage trail will commence even before the falls, rapid, or sharp bend can be seen. On well-traveled routes, these portages are likely to be clearly marked, but as one gets farther and farther from civilization, the signs may become more obscure and the penalty for a miscalculation more severe.

In the case of waterfalls, you had better have a good idea beforehand of the location of the portage.

Careful scouting of an otherwise questionable rapid may suggest several strategies, including the avoidance of a laborious portage. By carrying just the gear around the drop, your canoe is lightened and more maneuverable, and you have eliminated the risk of losing food and duffel. Then it is possible that two of your crew, considerably more skilled than the others, can paddle all the canoes through, to rendezvous with the rest of the crew at the bottom of the drop. For years, this was the strategy my wife and I employed with our young kids.

## Lining

Still another strategy, which is one of canoe tripping's most endearing techniques, is known as lining. Sometimes it just means wading and hauling the canoe through the shallower pools and drops at the perimeter of a rapid. In its purest form, lining consists of people at bow and stern, alternately pulling and yielding on lines attached to bow and stern, letting their loaded or unloaded canoe down a drop deemed otherwise unrunnable. Clarity of communication between partners and an understanding of the physics of water, boat, and line are absolutely essential to the success of the operation. Should the canoe be allowed to get broadside to the current, due to inattentiveness at the stern or

"Lining" a canoe often ends up as an exercise in wading.

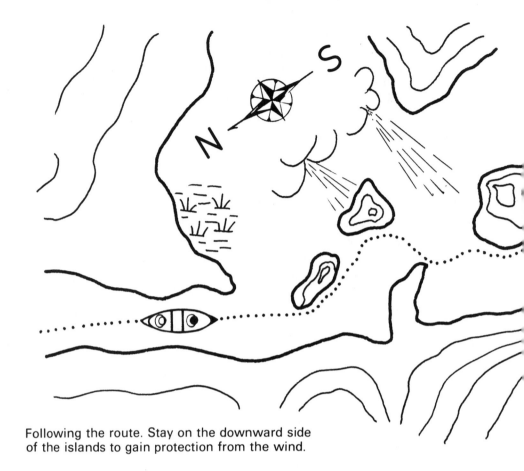

Following the route. Stay on the downward side
of the islands to gain protection from the wind.

excessive hauling in at the bow, catastrophe can only be averted by immediately
letting go of the stern line so that the canoe swings full around as the person
at the bow continues to hang on for dear life. Lining is often impractical where
there is a torturous shoreline, requiring the paddlers to go into the water up
to their waists or higher, sometimes hanging onto the canoe, sometimes using
the lines to restrain it.

## Other Navigation Problems

On a many-channeled river, you may have to choose the proper channel. It is
often not self-evident, but try to take the first and largest channel in terms of
volume. Often a wide but shallow channel will beckon promisingly, only to
peter out noisily through a gravel bar at the lower end of a midriver island.

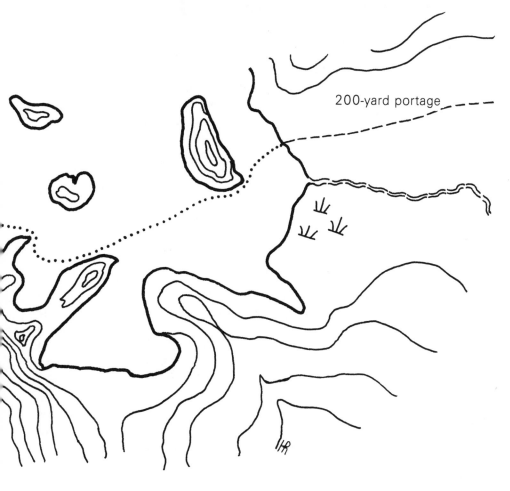

200-yard portage

Good humor is apt to be your ultimate salvation in any of these situations.

Finding your way down a sizable lake to locate either a stream outlet or portage presents different problems. Also, the presence or threat of wind or storm will affect your strategy. The navigational challenge is one of translating the two-dimensional map to a three-dimensional reality, seen from the constantly changing vantage point of the canoer. It's not as difficult as it sounds.

## Using Your Map

As you move north to south on the map, you will be counting off the reference points, your map spread out before you on the packs. An occasional check of the compass will keep you oriented, as you attain each "headland" or island. These reference points, in addition to deep bays or a prominent contour (perhaps a cliff or peak jutting above the surrounding topography), are constantly checked back against the map, as you strain to pick out the next distant headland. Although your course as the crow flies may lie directly to the south, a route designed to avoid the wind, by seeking the lee protection of points or islands, may take you on the zigzag course shown on the map. Attentiveness, rather than sophisticated navigation, will usually ensure success.

Your outlet is likely to be found in the obvious topographic depression discernible at the south end of the lake. The higher ground skirting the marshy outlet of an intermittent creek is the likely location of your portage. A weathered blaze on an old tree trunk and a grassy clearing trampled down by earlier parties are evidence that you have found it.

## The Portage Trail

The portage is much maligned, and unfairly so. It is work, to be sure, but the reward is a change of scene and new vistas. After several hours of paddling, the prospect of stretching the legs mingles with the anticipation of glimpsing a new body of water at trail's end. Too, several portages are likely to put you beyond the throngs of weekend paddlers. Indeed, it is the portage trail that makes possible a long and varied canoe trip carrying you across the watersheds, through the forest, and around falls and unrunnable rapids.

Being organized and knowing how to negotiate a portage can prevent an ordeal. If you know your route involves many portages, pack accordingly; more freeze-dried and lightweight food, fewer but larger packs, fewer changes of clothes, tents and bedding selected for lightness, and, most importantly, canoes no heavier than 75 pounds with a suitable yoke. Be stingy with the miscellaneous items. Count up the number of loads or packs (some may be carried two at a time), plus the canoes, and divide by the number in your crew. If the answer is more than two, try harder. Doubling a portage—that's two trips for one or more of the party—is fine, but if the portages are long or numerous, making three trips is laborious and time-consuming.

At the start of the portage trail, those with the heaviest packs, or the canoes, should be given some assistance. All loose gear should be consolidated to eliminate anyone's having to carry packs, tackle boxes, or cook pots in their hands. Paddles, if they are not being used as part of the carrying yoke, can be used as hiking staffs. Other than the bow and stern lines, try to refrain from stuffing odds and ends into the ends of the canoe; you'll upset the balance and exaggerate the weight (the lever principle again). If it's bug season, apply bug dope before you wed yourself to pack or canoe and head off down the trail.

Depending on the amount of traffic and the terrain, portages run the gamut

The portage trail is a part of canoe tripping.

from forest path to rocky staircase and gooey quagmire, sometimes all three on the same trail. It is often wise to test the length and condition of the trail with one of the lighter loads before staggering off with the canoe over your eyes. Once started, a good rule to follow is to "step over," not "on," rocks and logs.

Rest as frequently as need be. Another strategy is to carry one pack halfway across and then return for your second load, the return walk serving as a rest. The canoe carrier should be on the lookout for a friendly tree crotch —perhaps identified on the first trip—where the bow of the canoe can be wedged for a rest stop, without having to go through the much more strenuous exercise of getting the canoe up and down from the shoulders.

Perhaps the most important tactic on the portage trail is the encouraging word. A white lie, now and then, is permissible. "Keep moving, Dave. You're almost there." It's enough to keep you going, and there are few sensations to compare with that first glimpse of blue water as trail's end is neared.

## Finding and Choosing a Campsite

Campsites are either a result of planning or a refuge of expediency. The latter usually represents a plan gone awry. The intended campsite was no doubt chosen because its location coincided with your mileage-per-day estimates, a rumored fishing hole, the outfitter or diarist's glowing description, or because it was the last piece of dry ground before the route vanished into ten miles of swamp. One of the predictable things in canoe tripping is that trips seldom unfold as planned, but if predictability were your objective you would have stayed home and watched baseball. Thus, it should not unravel you when a windy lake, a wrong turn, or a balky crew prevents your party from achieving the planned mileage, meaning you will be searching for a bivouac of expediency.

Even if you reach the intended objective, it is possible that it will be occupied. Depending on the desperateness of the situation, the condition of your crew, and the lateness of the hour, you must decide whether or not to impose yourself—if the site can accommodate another party—sweat out the next ten miles, or backtrack to an undesirable but adequate site.

If you have no predetermined camps, be aware of another law of canoe tripping: The later the hour and the more tired the crew, the fussier they become in choosing a campsite. Start looking early—say around 3 P.M.—and if you see one that meets your basic needs, grab it. A lot of campsites of expediency have resulted from ignoring this law. Sometimes, it will be uncooperative Mother Nature that forces choice upon you. How often the wind has driven us to seek the nearest refuge, to make do, until the weather decided to release us.

Assuming you have a choice, what should you be looking for? Perfection is a breezy, bug-free point blessed by morning and evening sun and yet not so exposed as to be at the mercy of inclement weather. It is gently sloped to shed a heavy rain, high enough above the water so as not to be drowned in chill morning mists rising off the water, and of even disposition for the setting of tents and mats. Its ample open area provides a view and feeling of freedom while, nearby, a fine forest exudes wilderness and yields plenty of dry wood. Earlier canoers will have built an unobtrusive but utilitarian fireplace and left a small stack of dry wood for the next campers—you. That, in fact, will be the only evidence of their passing through.

A sandy beach or drop-off will invite you to swim or fish. Fresh water will be easily accessible from the camp kitchen. As evening falls, the haunting cry of the loon and the rising drone of night sounds will slowly envelop you and your companions. As the final embers of your campfire expire, one by one, your exhausted crew will retire to the warmth and security of their tents.

Finding the perfect campsite after a long day's paddle.

A gravel bar makes a fine campsite.

That's the way it is—sometimes. Often you will have to compromise. But perfection means different things to different people. The tantalizing rapids that promise great fishing to one member of the crew may be a noisy reminder to another, who tosses and turns throughout the night, knowing that in the morning they must be run. But the search for Shangri-la is one of the joys of canoe tripping, and memorable campsites are often the plot in the unfolding story, the paddling and portaging only a means to an end.

The following checklist is time-tested, but each person has different ideas about what's a necessity, so the list will be expanded or contracted depending on the individual. The important thing is to make a final check of your list and your outfit before you launch into the wilderness.

## Canoe Trip Checklist

*Clothing*

—full-brimmed or wool hat
—work gloves
—boots, waterproof or rubber-bottomed
—wool socks (or wool blend)
—denim or khaki long pants (one change)
—hiking shorts
—wool shirt
—PolarGuard vest
—rain suit or poncho
—underwear
—bandannas or handkerchiefs
—towel
—tennis shoes

*Tents and Bedding*

—tent with rain fly
—extra rain tarp
—sash cord or nylon line (for rigging rain tarps, etc.)
—down, PolarGuard, or Fiberfill sleeping bag
—foam mats (or air/foam such as Therma-Rest)

—nesting pots and pans with cups
—plastic bowls
—two-quart juice container
—knives, forks, spoons
—soup and coffee ladle
—large spoon
—spatula
—foil
—paper towels
—S.O.S. or Tuffy
—toilet paper
—stove
—candles or fire starter
—sharp heavy-duty knife
—tools (including goose-necked pliers for grabbing pots)
—folding saw and Hudson's Bay ax
—matches (in match safe or waterproof container)

## Canoe Equipment

—paddles (one extra for each canoe)
—PFDs
—bailer and sponge
—heavy line for lining, securing, throw rope
—maps, trip notes, and waterproof case
—compass

## Miscellaneous

—insect repellent
—biodegradable soap
—bug spray
—fishing rods and tackle
—camera and film
—paperback book
—notebook and pen
—shaving kit

# 10

# The Expedition

As recently as 1904, magazine writer Leonidas Hubbard and his companion, Dillon Wallace, a New York lawyer, dreamed of exploring by canoe the *terra incognita* of Labrador. Their trip came to pass, only to end in nightmare and the death by starvation of young Hubbard.

But today there are no blank spaces on the map of North America—or anywhere else, for that matter. Even those remote places touched only briefly by the explorer's foot have yielded to the satellite's searching eye or the geologist's magnetometer. Atavistic yearnings cause us to ponder the map and the possibilities, nonetheless. For some, a four-day canoe trip in the Ozarks of Missouri will satisfy the hunger. Others need longer canoe trips, to more remote places, until, one day, succumbing to the urge to test the limits of their outdoor and canoeing skills.

Despite civilization's pervasiveness, places still exist where the illusion, if not the actuality, of total aloneness can be experienced. Another kind of trip might touch inhabited areas in many places, but be of such duration and complexity— for example, crossing a continent—as to be, in every sense, an expedition.

The canoe expeditioner cuts the cord to so-

Large lakes require that the expeditioner be able to translate on a grand scale.

called creature comforts to pursue self-reliance, dreaming, researching, planning; finally bringing people, canoes, food, and gear together for a trip that, one hopes, will fall just short of being an "adventure" of the sort that arctic explorer Vilhjalmur Stefansson called a sign of bad planning.

## SKILLS

The requisites for a canoe expedition are imagination, curiosity, and skills to match. Beyond that, you will need one or more partners with similar appetites, compatible chemistry, and still more skill. Crew discord has torn asunder many a trip or, worse, endangered its participants.

It goes without saying that the expedition members should possess a high order of canoeing skills, but if you have a choice between good judgment and a good cross draw, go with the judgment. Although it is worthwhile to know *how* to run difficult rapids, it is essential to know *when not* to. There is an adage to the effect that "no Indian ever drowned on a portage." A wise crew weighs the objective elements of a given course, including water and air temperatures, time of day, and water levels, and also the subjective considerations of remoteness, the personality of the river, crew condition—both mental and physical—and the possible and probable consequences of a miscalculation.

Judgment is a product of experience. Having made progressively more difficult canoe trips, you and your crew should now have good canoeing and outdoor skills. In addition, longer and more remote travel calls for greater navigational ability, first-aid or medical training, and ingenuity in the selection of food, clothing, and gear. And physical conditioning in preparation for an expedition is paramount.

Generally, the most serious navigation challenges are the large lakes. The principles are no different from those described in chapter 9, but an experienced expeditioner is able to translate on a huge scale, even though unable to see the opposite shoreline or the extremity of an immense bay. Hugging a shoreline may be impractical, and calculated risks will be taken as the party strikes out across a broad reach of open water, bound for an almost indistinct headland. In the more northerly latitudes, the correct reading of the compass becomes quite difficult owing to magnetic variations from true north of 25 to 30 degrees and more in some areas (these variations are usually indicated in the map data).

A carefully selected first-aid kit and basic first-aid knowledge on the part of at least one crew member is advisable. Knowing how to deal with hypothermia, heat stroke, severe bleeding, unconsciousness, or a broken bone is at a premium when an expedition is far from medical help.

Food selection and preparation in the bush becomes a high art when a crew embarks on a prolonged wilderness journey. Weight becomes a more critical consideration, as do the nutritive requirements for fueling a 25- to 40-mile-a-day regimen. A diet providing a balance of fats, carbohydrates, some protein, and roughage is essential to physical and mental well-being. Getting that balance is going to mean including some whole foods—cheeses, bacon, compressed meats or sausage—that add to the weight, but a diet exclusively of freeze-dried fare would bankrupt your crew, nutritionally and monetarily. Knowing how to make bannock bread on the trail is almost a necessity for an extended voyage. Fish may supplement the diet, but don't count on catching them in planning the menus.

We have outfitted parties of six for almost a month with what we could fit in our canoes and carry on our backs. For extended trips, or for other reasons, parties have sometimes arranged for air drops and caches at remote points.

In most of North America today it would be difficult, if not illegal, to attempt to live off the land. Much of the game is protected, and even if it were not, hunting is out of tune with the spirit of canoeing. We should be battling to preserve ever-dwindling wildlife resources. In that same vein, guns should not be a part of the canoe expeditioner's equipment, either for hunting or misguided ideas of protection. The actual cases of mauling or attacks by "wild" animals are statistically insignificant. They probably involved extraordinary circumstances and would have occurred no matter how well armed the victim. As far as bodily harm, more fatalities occur in one year as a result of bee stings than all the bear attacks ever recorded.

A clean campsite, with food well secured and positioned (please, not in the tent), out of the reach of bears, raccoons, and squirrels, will be the canoer's best protection against wildlife. If it is impractical to suspend food packs from a tree, put them under an overturned canoe, well anchored. A tarp or poncho stretched over the packs with rocks holding down the corners is also useful. One thing seems clear: The more remote the trip, the less likely it is that you will have unwanted visits from local wildlife. A remote wilderness campsite will not have had enough prior use to have become associated with food leavings, nor is it as likely to encroach on the animals' territory. Your most serious adversaries, by far, will be the mosquito and blackfly. Expeditioners will be wise to carry high-potency repellents and, in extreme conditions, head nets.

Most of the canoes, clothing, and gear suitable for canoe tripping will serve for an expedition, but with an even greater premium on quality and reliability. Take gear that will survive, along with whatever it takes to repair it. Canoes should be larger, and full-length decks (spray decks) are well worth considering. Depending on the waters contemplated, a spray deck provides warmth in addition to protection from rain and heavy standing waves.

## RESEARCH AND LOGISTICS

Thorough research is your best safeguard against surprises. Use reliable maps and supplement them with firsthand accounts of prior expeditions, including those of early explorers. Corresponding or visiting with the members of earlier parties can clarify unclear or conflicting journal references; with luck, you can sit down with your source to mark your map with the locations of campsites, portages, dangerous obstacles, or points of interest. You will also want to know the weather and water levels prevailing during your informant's trip, in order to judge the relevance of descriptions of certain rapids or the location of portages (many routes have high- and low-water portages).

Getting to and from your points of access and egress (by definition, if it's easy, it's not an expedition) is going to be your greatest challenge and expense. In the Canadian wilds, we have employed cars, trains, float planes, wagons, and motor launches. Canoes have been shipped, often months beforehand, by truck, barge, float plane, and train, and sometimes, following the trip, they have had to winter on frozen wastes, until arrangements could be made to pick them up. Float planes, such as the Cessna 185, Twin Beech, Beaver, and Twin Otter, are the workhorses of the bush; depending on size, configuration, and local regulations, they can carry up to three canoes, outside or inside the plane. They are costly, since you rent the entire plane on an hourly basis for a round trip, including the empty backhaul, and you are invariably at the mercy of monopolistic and whimsical operators.

## THREE CHALLENGING VOYAGES

This barely scratches the surface, but perhaps a recounting of three extraordinary accomplishments will provide a more tantalizing glimpse of the challenge and excitement of the expeditioner's experience.

## The Hoyt-Gregg-Lentz-Perry Back River Expedition

It is remarkable that in 1962 there could still be an enormous river system in North America, draining a million square miles of Canada's Northwest Territories, mostly treeless, whose waters had not seen a white man pass in over one hundred years. Called by the Indians Thlew-ee-choh-dezeth, or Great Fish River, it was first explored by an English Navy captain, George Back, and his crew of twelve in 1834.

Back's powerful description of his perilous descent of the river that now bears his name, with its tales of hairbreadth escapes and ungodly weather—including ice still blocking the oceanlike expanses of Pelly Lake in mid-July—adequately explains the paucity of tourists. Only a handful of canoers have made the trip in recent years—after the trailblazing Hoyt-Lentz expedition—and even so, the river is known to have claimed the lives of three persons.

In 1962, Hoyt and his team of paddlers drove almost four thousand miles to reach Yellowknife, capital of the Northwest Territories, before being flown 250 miles into the headwaters of the river. They would paddle 18-foot wood-and-canvas canoes and be on the river for forty-one days. A food cache had to be flown into the one-third point. Preparations for the trip took almost a full

Sometimes the only way out is by float plane.

year, including close study of maps and aerial photographs and careful reading of the journals of Captain Back and his lieutenant, James Anderson, of the Hudson's Bay Company, who descended the river in 1855. They found the river unchanged from Back's time, for the land is virtually uninhabited and without permanent settlement of any kind.

It is often the case that the most dangerous falls and rapids are passed uneventfully, while near-calamity strikes unexpectedly in seemingly innocuous places. Lentz and his partner had scouted a certain rapid and deemed it runnable, including one chute on the opposite side of the river which looked like so many others. Too late, Lentz and his bowman suddenly realized that their "chute" was actually a three-foot waterfall. Over they plunged, and in an instant both were immersed in 45-degree water whose force and velocity were deceptively powerful. Lentz, who was not wearing his life preserver at the time, was able to grab it as he went over, but it was only marginally useful as the river accelerated and widened. Numbed by the chill waters, Lentz began to lose both his will and his strength. Perhaps only the ignominy of drowning in water whose bottom was visible to him the entire time, and the timely arrival of the other canoe (which had taken a more propitious course), saved Lentz from an untimely demise. His bowman fared somewhat better. Lentz was treated for hypothermia by being put in one of the dry sleeping bags. He recovered quickly, relieved to have lost only a few personal articles.

There were apparently some sharp moments in the Hoyt-Lentz expedition, but the participants averred afterward that they would be willing to do it again with the same crew—usually a good sign. Several parties have followed Hoyt, Gregg, Lentz, and Perry, including the first all-Canadian team, in 1972, and the first women, in 1975. Not a river to be tackled lightly, the Back is probably unique in North American canoeing and offers a last opportunity to experience absolute remoteness in North America. We must be grateful to Captain Back, and to the hardy souls who rediscovered the river in 1962, for showing us the way.

## Kruger and Waddell, 7,000 miles from Montreal to the Bering Sea

In 1971, two ordinary men carried out an extraordinary plan and the realization of an ambitious dream. Verlen Kruger, a plumbing contractor from Lansing, Michigan, and Clint Waddell, a forestry technician, paddled a home-crafted canoe 6,717 miles from Montreal to the Bering sea in 176 days. They followed, for the most part, the 150-year-old routes of the voyageurs of the fur trade,

A large-volume C-2 runs an arctic river.

completing the trip in a single season. Only one other party is known to have succeeded in tracing a similar route. Geoffrey W. Pope and Sheldon P. Taylor, in two seasons, 1936 and 1937, canoed from New York City to Nome, Alaska.

The pace maintained by Kruger, forty-six years old at the time, and Waddell, thirty-six, was only slightly less vigorous than that which the two men had employed as a marathon racing team, where they had mastered the physical and psychological problems associated with prolonged exertion and going without sleep. Once under way, they found that they reached a plateau and were able to keep to their rigorous schedule without undue hardship. Despite their seemingly machinelike pace, they found time to enjoy the sights and sounds and to document the trip thoroughly with film and journal. In fact, they found time, en route, to enter a 250-mile canoe race in Flin Flon, Manitoba. They finished fifth!

Careful planning was certainly one key to their success. Kruger says that they devoted almost as many hours to research and planning as they did to paddling. Their canoe was designed and built by Kruger, using design precepts learned on the marathon racing circuit. It was of cedar strip construction, fiberglassed; 21 feet long and 34 inches at the beam. It had a detachable waterproof-nylon deck, weighed 85 pounds, and was fitted out with a portage yoke for one-man carrying. There were rapids to be run, but this was a canoe designed to make time on big lakes and big water, a right decision based on careful examination of the route and weighing of alternative compromises.

No fancy or expensive freeze-dried fare for this crew. They had learned that the fuel necessary for such an endeavor was basic carbohydrates, supplemented by moderate amounts of protein and fats. Oatmeal, trail-baked bannock, pancakes, potatoes, and rice were staples that could be bought off any grocery shelf. Inexpensive and available! They tried to assure themselves of three meals a day, as well as 15- to 20-minute snack stops every two to three hours. They could carry about two weeks' food provisions, which was sufficient to get them between outposts.

The entire trip, including 120 portages totaling 150 miles, was made without motorized assistance, and the questionable hospitality of most of the outposts was bypassed. The expeditioners preferred to camp beyond the sight and sound of semi-civilization, which, in the bush, is often more ramshackle than rustic.

One element sets this accomplishment apart from those of other celebrated expeditioners: the apparent lack of personal friction between Waddell and Kruger over this extended and arduous journey. Kruger offers a partial explanation. He chose as a partner a man who wanted, more than anything else, to make this journey, a man with whom he had already shared the rigors of the long-distance paddler, under the stress of competition.

The Kruger-Waddell expedition truly serves as an inspiration to today's canoer and speaks eloquently of the canoe's tremendous mobility. It also reminds us that the spirit of adventure is very much alive and that there still exist opportunities for spectacular achievements in an age of satiety.

## Greg and Cathy Jensen's All-American Transcontinental Route

It seems axiomatic that a new marriage should not be tested by even a two-week canoe trip, much less a seven-month 4,900-mile odyssey. Yet newlyweds Greg and Cathy Jensen put a hole in this cherished theory of mine, while accomplishing an effort worthy of any serious canoer's admiration. Leaving Astoria, Oregon, in May 1979, they paddled up the Columbia and Flathead rivers, breaching the Rockies at Cut Bank Pass; traveled for 2,000 miles down the Missouri to St. Louis; and canoed parts of the Mississippi, Ohio, and Tennessee rivers. At Bryson City, North Carolina, they made the portage over the Appalachians and worked their way down the Savannah River. On December 12, they reached the waters of the Atlantic.

For many of us who have written off much of our nation's waterways as having been lost to the dam builders, the trip is something of a revelation. Yes, the Jensens rode through the locks on the Columbia, portaged around some formidable dams, and crossed some oceanlike reservoirs, but they also traversed a diversity of wild and populated country. They derived as much satisfaction from their contacts with civilization and commerce—such as barge and riverboat traffic along the Mississippi—as they did from the more isolated and semi-wilderness areas on their journey. Traveling at a canoe's pace, they could absorb the rich history of an expanding frontier America. For much of the way they were retracing the route of Lewis and Clark.

The Jensens used an 18-foot aluminum canoe and a lightweight pyramid-style nylon backpacking tent; according to Cathy Jensen, "The rest of the equipment list would read like a garage-sale ad." They did their marketing along the route, and their diet largely depended on what stores they found. A well-stocked grocery store in a larger town meant a week of more sumptuous dining. The simplicity of their outfit—they hiked over Cut Bank Pass in sneakers—and their ability to provision themselves along the way is perhaps a message for some of us equipment freaks of the world and says much about travel by canoe.

# 11

## Competition

Competition canoeing in its many forms is growing rapidly in popularity but is still in its infancy. Until very recently, it has enjoyed greater status in Europe than in this country. This is particularly true for white-water events, inasmuch as Olympic flat-water paddling has been part of the U.S. scene for over fifty years. It is also ironic, considering the North American origins of the Eskimo kayak and the Indian canoe. However, this is all changing as more and more canoeists are trying their hand at the variety of competitive events open to them.

### WHY COMPETE?

For many people, competition gives purpose to their sport by creating the need for training or simply showing them how they stack up. Whether your goal is physical fitness or ego gratification, there is no question that competition sharpens the senses and skills that will stand you in good stead in other phases of the sport. The slalom racer forced to turn where the gate is, rather than at will, is going to be a more proficient recreational boater, and the occasional marathon participant is

175

A C-1 runs a forward gate.

not likely to be intimidated by a 30-mile day on a canoe trip.

For the canoer with serious aspirations, particularly in white-water competition, it is an "open" sport, requiring no club affiliation, and without an intricate maze of "seeding" or qualifying criteria. All that's required is a boat, paddles, and a partner. Increasingly, however, the weekend paddler and some-time racer is being superseded by the full-time disciplined specialist.

Interestingly, there may be an inverse correlation between exciting and plentiful water and the enthusiasm directed toward competitive activity. The heartland of the Midwest, where there is plenty of placid if unexciting water, is the focus of intense and broad participation in flat-water and marathon racing. The Pacific Northwest boasts an incredible variety of white water but produces very few national, much less world-class, paddlers; while the Washington, D.C.–based Canoe Cruisers Association, in the shadow of a metropolis and with a thin selection of rivers, produces an abundant crop. Obviously the challenge of competition can be a more than adequate substitute for limited natural-water thrills.

## History

International canoeing competitions, usually downriver races, began in Europe in the early 1920s, and in 1932, the first slalom race, a local affair, was held on the flat waters of Lake Hallwil in Switzerland. Just a year later the first white-water slalom was held on the Aar River in Switzerland, with the first National Championship held the following year. There, the paddlers negotiated buoys rather than today's suspended slalom gates.

## BOAT CLASSIFICATIONS

The sport of "canoeing" actually embraces both kayaks and canoes. In fact, the British, when they use the term canoeing, are more likely to be referring to kayaking, and a majority of the boats competing under the auspices of the International Canoe Federation are also kayaks. Put simply, the sport is canoeing; the boats come in different shapes and sizes.

Olympic flat-water boats, both canoes and kayaks, are a different breed, looking more like racing shells and demanding very specialized paddling techniques. The boats likely to be seen in your local or international white-water events will be organized, announced, and reported as K-1, K-1W (men's and women's solo kayak), and C-1, C-2, C-1W, C-2W, C-2M (single and double canoes for men, women, and mixed). The prefix "O" is added for "open," so that OC-2M designates an open, two-place canoe, paddled by a man and a woman.

Within the international flat-water and white-water classes and the broader classifications sanctioned by the American Canoe Association (ACA), there are continually evolving specifications meant to define and limit the designs of particular boats for particular events, such as width, length, some ratio of dimensions, etc. Events such as slalom or downriver races for open canoes which have been converted to white-water boats by means of temporary decking are also added as demand arises—a sign of a healthy, growing sport. And, finally, the race organizer, at whim, may further expand, limit, or define eligible boats and classes (aluminum canoes only, seniors, father-son, juniors, novices, etc.), to separate the obviously recreational designs from the not so obviously hotter boats and to attract a broader range of participants.

# TYPES OF COMPETITION

## Olympic Flat-water Competition

In flat-water competition, canoes and kayaks specially designed and regulated by Olympic rules are paddled by one, two, or four persons and raced over distances of 500 to 10,000 meters, usually on water with no current.

## White-water Competition

For white-water competition, two formats are used: slalom and wild-water (sometimes called downriver). The slalom competition takes place on a course defined by gates which must be negotiated in a prescribed sequence. Normally incorporated are downstream, forward, and reverse gates and upstream, forward, and reverse gates, numbering, in total, 25 to 30. Slalom racers make two runs and are ranked by their best run. Speed is important, but penalty time, ranging from 10 to 50 seconds for "touched" or missed gates, is added to elapsed time, to arrive at the aggregate time for the run.

A wild-water or downriver race is a race against time over a distance of 3 to 6 kilometers and on water of at least Class III difficulty. Most of the competing boats are closed, or decked, canoes and kayaks with severe V hulls and needlelike prows, but there is open canoe competition in the event as well. Like a downhill ski racer, the paddler must seek the "best line" down the river.

An intriguing variation on the downriver theme is the true chariot race

Leaving an upstream gate in a slalom course, this C-2 must now peel down river (right).

of canoeing, where open canoes race over flat and white water for distances of anywhere from 5 to 40 miles, often involving several portages. These are good tests of overall canoemanship, with all the uncertainty of a backgammon game.

## Marathon Racing

Not as well defined as the runner's counterpart, marathon canoe racing takes place over courses of 5 to 70 miles in length on water usually no more difficult than Class I or II. Depending on the race, it may be open to canoes and kayaks, both open and closed, aluminum canoes, and open canoes of 16 feet or less, and divided into classes, such as men's, women's, and mixed. Sometimes included are classes for so-called "pro-boats," incorporating more severe racing hulls defined under both International Canoe Federation and United States Canoe Association rules. Length, width, and ratios of length and width at given water line are closely controlled, and these boats are immediately recognizable by their low profiles, precarious freeboard, adjustable seats and foot braces, and

Trying out a Pro boat and bent-shaft paddles. It's a super-light, high-performance racing boat for flat water.

often asymmetrical hulls. They're powered by serious paddlers working on a prearranged cadence. "Hut! Hut! Hut!" they chant in teutonic precision, stroking at 60 beats per minute with bent short paddles and changing sides every 6 to 8 strokes. For these zealots, correcting strokes are an abhorrence.

For every race attracting the "pro-boat," however, there are a dozen representing the equivalent of a "fun run," open to canoes of all shapes and sizes and to paddlers of all sexes, ages, and abilities. Then there are the hybrids! For a number of years, the city of Bellingham, Washington, has sponsored a "Ski to Sea" relay race, which in the past three years has attracted over 125 teams, ranging from hackers to national champions. Each team is made up of a downhill skier, a runner, a biker, and a canoeing pair and covers a nearly 70-mile course, starting with the skiers, 6,000 feet up on imposing Mount Baker, and ending with the canoers on the tidal lower reaches of the Nooksack River. Taking the final baton, the canoers battle for three hours or more to complete the final 30-mile relay leg. Prizes for the top teams, and plenty of cold beer for all, make for a unique, exhilarating, and fun-filled event.

There are many canoe races that are the equivalent of a fun run.

## Poling

Years ago on the Allagash, I had the opportunity to be instructed in canoe poling by an honest-to-goodness Maine guide. He had been poling his way up and down rivers for 50 years. Several hours were spent practicing all he had taught me, but I never really mastered the techniques. My mentor gave me a graduation present, anyway; a hand-hewn, 12-foot-long maple pole, with a soft metal shoe on one end, which was designed to get a purchase on the river bottom without getting stuck.

I still haven't mastered poling and my prized graduation present resides unused in the garage. The advent of tougher canoes, advanced paddling techniques and roads leading to many more upstream put-ins seems to have largely made the pole obsolete. The old-time poler was able to work his way up swift rivers to destinations accessible by no other means. Standing with his feet wide-based, one a little ahead of the other, the pole was planted off the upstream gunwale. By moving hand-over-hand up the pole, he could propel the canoe upstream, working the slower moving, shallower waters at the edge of the river, maneuvering in and out of the eddies, and ferrying the canoe in either direction by constantly adjusting the angle of the canoe to the current. Returning down-river, the accomplished poler would "snub" the canoe, stopping, moving over, letting the canoe down through the trickiest drops.

Some of us may have put away our pole, but the art has been revived in the form of a competitive activity by a growing band of dedicated practitioners. Since 1975, national poling championships sanctioned by the A.C.A. have permitted competitors to test their agility, speed, endurance, and water-reading skills. Using lightweight aluminum poles and perfected techniques, they can perform feats of upstream and downstream travel that the old-timers would admire, and which would put a mere paddler to shame.

Poling may indeed be due for new popularity based on its original, practical merits. Its adherents rightly point out that it opens up a whole new world of little streams and rivers and their headwaters, where the poler may escape the weekend crowds on popular rivers. Unexplored stretches can be scouted from below without fear of being swept down a sudden drop. If insurmountable obstacles are encountered by the upstream explorer, he or she may simply turn around and drift back downriver to the put-in. That's another attraction. There is no shuttle. Fuel consumption is slashed and the time used to move cars back and forth is spent on the water.

Since they are no longer making old-time Maine guides, especially outside of Maine, the aspiring canoe poler may have to do a little research to find either a pole or an instructor. A local canoe club affiliated with the A.C.A. is probably the best place to start.

# 12

# Motorized Canoes

Canoeing is best enjoyed as a self-propelled sport, but to entirely shun the motor is to deny the versatility of the canoe. The motor's noise and smell may be an unnatural match for the canoe, but there are times when a marriage of convenience can be the answer to a special need. Despite the weight of motor and gas (five gallons weighs almost 25 pounds), which might slow you down on a portage, a 2½ hp motor can be a veritable lake eater, enabling you to cover three to four times the distance possible with paddles alone.

The motor might be accessory to a trip whose primary focus was fishing or photography, and where the time required to reach a distant target did not permit the leisure of paddling. It could be used by a large family group to reach a base camp beyond the crowded, close-in waters; after which the canoers could resort to self-propulsion for making their daily forays to fish, photograph, or explore. For a trip intended to be primarily by paddle, one motor can be used to tow the entire party (we have towed as many as five fully loaded canoes using one 2½ hp outboard) up a large, heavily trafficked lake, to put both lake and people behind us before commencing on the canoe trip proper. Finally, an entire canoe trip with two or

183

Towing canoes behind a motor launch
may give your canoe trip a head start.

three canoes could employ the services of one small outboard (and provision for towing) to make an extended trip, difficult by paddle alone.

The motor should not be a substitute for paddles, but it can save many miles of head-down slogging and allow the freedom to paddle and explore those stretches of water that appeal to the trippers. Motorized canoeing is definitely not a way to beat wind and waves. Against a moderate headwind the motor is a boon, but when whitecaps appear, head for shore, either to determine a strategy employing paddles or patiently sit it out. The relentless push of the motor on rough water is no substitute for two paddlers riding with the waves, adjusting their strokes and body action to the seas beneath them. In short, if you can't paddle it, don't motor it.

## The Motor Mount

There are square-ended canoes obviously designed to take a motor. Less obvious is the fact that a motor squeezed onto the narrow end of such a canoe, with its handle poking into the small of the stern rider's back, is an awkward arrangement, to say the least. Preferable is a standard canoe using a well-designed motor mount which puts motor and handle alongside the person in the stern, eliminating the need to twist around or grope for a handle behind you. The compromise is, of course, that the motor offset to one side is going to require counterbalancing by positioning both packs and paddlers for proper trim.

There are commercially available motor mounts that are adaptable to all canoe models. Look for an adjustable one that can be clamped securely to the

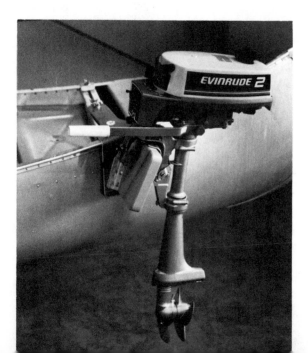

A small motor mounted to the side of the stern seat is an effective lake eater.

A tow harness using a giant bowline around the hull and a paddle for quick release prevents "hogging" by the towed canoe.

gunwale with a minimum of fuss. A hardwood or marine-plywood mounting block completes the requirements.

## Size

Small electric motors are extremely light and quiet, but the battery pack is heavy and cumbersome if any portaging is required. A small gas outboard of less than 5 hp is the best bet. Find a gas can of undoubted integrity too; despite deft handling, gasoline and its fumes have a way of permeating everything within seventeen feet of it. Many engines require a gas-oil mixture, so be sure you know the proportions before you get into the bush, and make sure the gas is kept free of dirt and sand and filtered for good measure. A screwdriver, small wrench, plenty of shear pins, and crossed fingers should prepare you for the inevitable snags and rocks.

## Towing

If two or more canoes are involved, you will need a good towing harness. Do not attempt to tow using the normal bow and stern rings on the canoe since this will cause the following canoe to "hog," or swing back and forth in whiplike fashion. Instead, make a giant loop with a bowline knot and slide it over the bow of the canoe, positioning the knot directly under the keel line. If the canoe to be towed is loaded, the weight should be slightly toward the stern, which will also help the canoe to plane rather than hog. Inserting the paddle blade through your giant bowline and under the front seat or thwart holds the loop in place and allows for quick dismantlement, in an emergency or otherwise. If you are going to be towing your own party, the passengers can be in their normal positions in the following canoes with the stern paddlers on the alert, using paddles as occasional rudders to maintain alignment.

## Portaging

If you are going to be facing some portages, take along a pack frame to which you can fasten motor, mount, and gas can to carry across as a separate load. Do not attempt to portage the canoe with the mount still attached, since it will tend to grab every passing bush, and those few pounds at the end of the canoe are the equivalent of twenty additional pounds square on your back. Likewise, trying to carry motor and gas can like suitcases is awkward and tiring for all but the shortest portages.

It is worth repeating that you should not attempt to motor on water you would not paddle, nor should you plan a canoe trip around a motor. Canoers should choose the trip and determine the utility of the motor after all the imponderables and variables have been considered. I would also be hesitant to take a trip where I had to rely on a motor to get me there and back, inasmuch as modern inventions have a way of breaking down at inopportune moments; in other words, the total mileage should always be a distance that could be paddled, even if at a considerable cost in time and physical effort.

# Afterword

## A Plea for the Waterways

In 1974, Americans experienced for the first time a shortage in a commodity they had come to take for granted—had, in fact, come to depend on—oil. We have also taken for granted another and far more priceless asset—our water resources. Industrialization, power, irrigation, flood control, harvests, mineral extraction, land development, population pressure—all wage a relentless battle against our waterways, and the waterways are losing.

The analogy with oil is all too valid. We have never set a proper value on our water resources and have squandered them accordingly. It is not uncommon to discover that, from time to time, certain of our rivers have had 110 percent of their annual average flow allocated to various users. Often the worthy purpose is irrigation, so that farming is encouraged on arid land where only the availability of cheap water makes agriculture possible.

The natural and perennial flooding of certain rivers provides the excuse for politicians to promote still more pork-barrel dam-building projects rather than pursue undramatic flood-plain zoning. An entire bureaucracy is kept busy looking for new dam sites. In the name of flood control,

187

power, and recreation (usually meaning motorboats), dams and their associated impoundments are built. The result is that only a handful of rivers are left in the United States where one can travel for more than a few days without encountering some man-made obstruction; fewer still, where the traveler will find some semblance of the primitive state. Unfortunately, much of the work of man is irreversible.

In 1967—and none too soon—the Wild and Scenic Rivers Act was passed by Congress, designating twenty-seven candidates for possible inclusion and setting a ten-year schedule for determining which rivers would qualify. The process is agonizingly slow. Studies are not begun until several years after they are authorized, and then it takes as long as four or five years to complete a report. Nevertheless, progress has been made, and the national system now includes about 2,300 miles on 28 stretches of river, with 841 miles classified as wild, 774 as scenic, and 702 as recreational. These classifications are defined as follows:

*Wild:* Unpolluted, undammed, and primitive surroundings accessible only by trails

*Scenic:* Undammed, with shoreline largely undeveloped, accessible by road

*Recreational:* Readily accessible, with some development and pre-existing dams allowed

Despite this progress, the number of protected waterways is minimal compared to those irretrievably lost through years of neglect and exploitation. At the same time, river use by canoers, kayakers, and rafters (both commercial and private) is escalating at a phenomenal rate. In the period 1970 to 1976, the number of rafters, canoeists, and kayakers on the Youghiogheny in Pennsylvania leaped from 17,000 to 95,500. Here, and on the Potomac in Maryland, boaters must literally queue up to gain access to the river or enter a rapid.

On popular western rivers, such as the Colorado, the Rogue and the Salmon, one must have a permit to run, and a battle rages between commercial rafters, who have the lion's share of the permit allocations, and private boaters, who sometimes must wait years to run them.

Rafting, particularly as it has escalated to its most rapacious commercial forms, has given hundreds of thousands of curious, well-heeled adventurers a taste of white-water excitement, but they are missing the essential element of intimacy. Unlike solitary and tandem canoeists, who must deal with every whim and truculence of a busily descending river and who live by the fruits or penalties of their execution, rafters are more of a tour group who have placed themselves in the hands of a tour director.

Our waterways are a scarce resource which requires protection.

In the popular canoe-tripping areas, the influx of enthusiastic but environmentally thoughtless legions of canoers has created sanitation, litter, and waterway degradation problems. Too late, we have discovered how little remains to be enjoyed in a semi-wild or pristine state. Then, too, many have rushed to take to the waters and the trails before fully understanding the safe and sane pursuit of the sport, and often without an appreciation or knowledge of living in nondestructive harmony with the wilderness environment. In this sense, at least, the permit system—where it exists—has been the savior of certain waterways. Strict regulation has meant that one can pull into camp on the Middle Fork of the Salmon, for example, and be scarcely aware that a dozen people camped on that same site the previous night, and perhaps every night for the past two weeks.

As discouraging as this may sound, the situation is far from hopeless. And there are certainly many thousands of miles of water where the canoeist can enjoy solitude, history, and scenic beauty—if not untamed wilderness. But the battle must be fought vigorously on the political front by a growing constituency of paddlers who would preserve as much of what remains as possible, and endeavor, as well, to reclaim whatever may be salvageable. Our water resources, and the vast network of lakes and rivers upon which our country grew and was nurtured, is worth preserving—for those who paddle today and for our children and grandchildren, who should not be denied this priceless part of our North American heritage.